The History of Heathrow

Philip Sherwood

Hillingdon Libraries 1990

ISBN 0907869-270

Rev. Ed. 1993

© P.T.Sherwood 1990
Designed by Publicity and Marketing Section
London Borough of Hillingdon Published by
Hillingdon Libraries, Central Library, High Street,
Uxbridge. and printed by Echo Press (1983) Ltd.,
Loughborough

FOREWORD

There are many accounts of Heathrow, mostly written by civil aviation enthusiasts. This book is not for them and such enthusiasts should read no further. It is written from the point of view of someone who has seen the former pleasant and peaceful countryside of West Middlesex destroyed in less than fifty years. This change from a largely agricultural area to the world's busiest international airport is often referred to as progress - a word which the dictionary defines as, "an advance to something better or later in development". Anybody who can remember what the Heathrow area was like before the advent of the airport will surely agree that progress is hardly the appropriate word.

My original intention was to write an account of what the Heathrow area used to be like to supplement two pictorial publications (see references 1 and 2) of which I was joint editor, and Part I of this book is this account. However, in the hope of possibly finding more photographic material a search was made of Air Ministry files now deposited in the Public Record Office. These produced no photographs, but they did bring to light disturbing details of how and why the airport came about.

The claim has always been made that Heathrow was developed as a result of an urgent need for the RAF to have a bomber base in the London area. The files in the PRO show that there was never such a need and the airfield was regarded from the start as being a civil airport for London. The War Cabinet was deceived into giving approval for the development, even although it meant diverting resources away from the war-effort at a time when preparations were being made for the Normandy landings. The Defence of the Realm Act 1939 was used by the Air Ministry to requisition the land and to circumvent the public inquiry that would otherwise have had to be held. Part 2 of the book therefore describes the results of the examination of the files that show the true story behind the development.

The development of the airport has totally changed the social structure of the communities living around it. Many of these are now dependent on the airport for their economic well-being and resent any criticism of it. However, as relative newcomers they should accept that there are some who are even more resentful of the manner in which the airport came about. They are in any case outnumbered by those who live within earshot of Heathrow who derive no benefit from it but are reminded every minute of the day of its presence.

The fact that Heathrow plays a vital role in the national economy cannot be questioned, but the major British airport would be bound to play such a role wherever it was situated. The argument against Heathrow as the site for the major airport is that it was singularly ill-chosen and the development should not have taken place by what was little short of fraud. Ever since that ill-fated decision in 1943 the rights of people have been subordinated to the interests of civil aviation, to the point where one could say of Heathrow as Goldsmith wrote in his poem "The Deserted Village" - *"Ill fares the land, to hast'ning ills a prey, where wealth accumulates and men decay."*

P.T.Sherwood
Harlington 1989

ACKNOWLEDGEMENTS

Grateful thanks are due to:

Mr.William Wild for permission to include the description of Heathrow as recalled by his father, the late Mr.David Wild.

Miss Mary Pearce and Mr R. Westwood for assistance in the editing and preparation of the final text.

Mrs Jane Wood for compiling the index.

Mr.J.Marshall for providing the information on model aircraft flying at Heathrow and for making Figures 8, 9 and 13 available.

Mr.J.Chinery for making available the correspondence between Sir Richard Fairey and Sir Clive Baillieu and to the organisations listed below for permission to reproduce the following figures:

Figure 1. Quadrant/Flight International.

Figure 15. West Drayton and District Local History Society.

Figure 21. Hayes and Harlington Local History Society.

Figures 16 and 17 are Crown copyright material in the Public Record Office and are reproduced by permission of the Controller of HMSO.

Figure 23 is based on Crown copyright material and is also reproduced by permission of the Controller of HMSO.

All other figures are in the public domain or are the author's own copyright.

THE HISTORY OF HEATHROW

CONTENTS Page

Foreword 3
Acknowledgements 5
Introduction 9

PART 1
FROM PREHISTORIC TIMES UNTIL 1943 11
Topography 11
Prehistory 13
General Roy and King's Arbour 14
The hamlet of Heathrow 16
Agriculture 18
Other Industry 20
The Perry Oaks Sludge Works 20
Gravel Digging 20
The Fairey Aerodrome 20
A walk round Heathrow in 1935 24

PART 2
THE DEVELOPMENT OF THE AIRPORT 1943 - 1951 35
The origins of the development 35
Factors inhibiting the development 37
The Perry Oaks problem 37
The problem of the Fairey aerodrome 38
The noise problem 39
Agricultural considerations 40
The fate of the inhabitants 41
Other problems 45
The stages of development 46

PART 3
DEVELOPMENTS 1952 - 1988 53
Ancillary developments 53
The fourth terminal 55
The fifth terminal 56
The pressures for further development 58
Airport expansion 58
Surface access 60
Epilogue. 61

Postscript 63

REFERENCES 72
INDEX 74

ILLUSTRATIONS

Page

Figure 1. Aerial view of Heathrow in 1935 — 11
Figure 2. Ordnance Survey Map of Heathrow 1935. — 12
Figure 3. Heathrow area 1754 (from Rocque's map of Middlesex). — 13
Figure 4. Caesar's Camp 1723. — 14
Figure 5. NW terminal of General Roy's baseline. — 17
Figure 6. The Thames Valley Market Gardening Plain 1936. — 19
Figure 7. Ploughing Match at Heathrow 1935. — 19
Figure 8. Flying Programme of Royal Aeronautical Society 1939. — 21
Figure 9. Annual Gala meeting of Model Flying Club. — 22
Figure 10. The "Three Magpies", Bath Road. — 24
Figure 11. Heathrow Hall 1935. — 25
Figure 12. Modern Farmhouses at Heathrow 1944. — 26
Figure 13. Duke of Northumberland's River 1937. — 29
Figure 14. Cottages at Heathrow 1935. — 29
Figure 15. Perry Oaks Farm 1937. — 30
Figure 16. Initial Proposals for the Airport 1943. — 47
Figure 17. Proposals for the extended airport 1946. — 48
Figure 18. Modified proposals for the extended airport 1950. — 50
Figure 19. Ash Cottage, Harlington Corner 1967. — 54
Figure 20. Ibis Hotel, Harlington Corner 1988. — 54
Figure 21. "Coach and Horses" and Ariel Hotel, 1961. — 55
Figure 22. Post House Hotel 1988. — 56
Figure 23. Possible location for a new runway at Heathrow and a railway link with Paddington — 60

INTRODUCTION

Heathrow today is known world-wide as the main international airport for London. This is a development which has occurred only in the last 45 years and before this it was an obscure hamlet in West Middlesex that had existed as such for about 700 years. Part 1 of this account traces its history from prehistoric times up to the development which, although it retains the same name, completely buried under the concrete the fields and farmsteads that once occupied the area.

In Part 2 the events leading up to the development of the airport are described from the time it was first proposed in 1943 to the abandonment in 1951 of the proposed extension north of the Bath Road. Part 3 covers further developments that have occurred with proposals to extend the airport from 1951 to the present.

Figures in brackets refer to references on page 63.

PART 1

FROM PREHISTORIC TIMES UNTIL 1943

TOPOGRAPHY

Heathrow is in a part of the Thames valley in which over the course of several million years the Thames has gradually moved southwards. During periods of glaciation followed by subsequent thaw the river must have been flowing at such a speed that it was able to carry gravels from the glaciers and

Fig 1. Aerial view of Heathrow in 1935 (reproduced by permission Quadrant/Flight International)

Fig 2. Ordnance Survey Map of Heathrow 1935

icefields to the north and west. Fast flowing water can carry clay and silt much more easily than gravel, so that when the flow rate decreased, as the river approached the sea, the gravel would have been deposited first. As the sea level rose with the melting of the ice the flow rate decreased still further and allowed the clay and silt to settle out on top of the gravel previously deposited. This layer dried out as the river retreated to give the brickearth deposits which overlie the gravel in many parts of the Thames valley. The fact that the gravel and the overlying soils were deposited under water means that the land is flat and level in character with a general slope of no more than ten feet per mile (Figure 1).

The Heathrow area occupies the south-east corner of Harmondsworth parish with the Bath Road forming a convenient boundary between it and the rest of the parish (see Figure 2). On the geological map the Bath Road also happens to follow (probably not by chance) the boundary between the brickearth deposits to the north and the Taplow terrace gravel deposits to the south. This does not mean that there is an abrupt change at this boundary, but the thickness of the brickearth overlying the gravel (which can be as much as three feet in thickness to the north of the Bath Road) becomes gradually reduced in a southerly and easterly direction. Towards the extreme south-east of the parish the soil covering is very thin and was part of Hounslow Heath, which had a soil described by Cobbett (3) on one of his rural rides as, " *a nasty strong dirt upon a bed of gravel and is a sample of all that is bad and villainous in look*". For good measure Cobbett considered that the labouring people of this area, "*looked to be about half Saint Giles's, dirty and had every appearance of drinking gin*".

Page 12

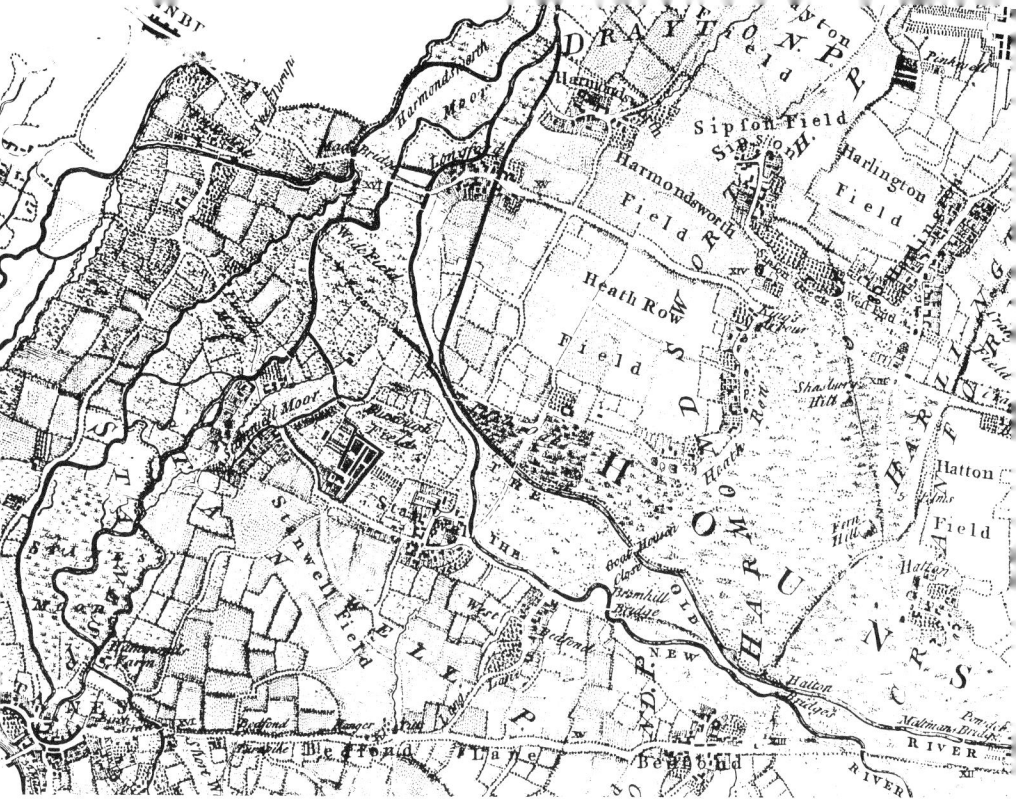

Fig 3. Heathrow area 1754 (from Rocque's map of Middlesex)

PREHISTORY

The villages and hamlets of West Middlesex, if not of Anglo-Saxon origin, certainly have Anglo-Saxon place names, but long before Saxon times there were settlements in the area. No written record exists but there is plenty of archaeological evidence for human occupation (4). The most significant in the Heathrow area was the discovery during the construction of the airport of an extensive iron-age settlement.

Pre-war Ordnance Survey maps show a rectangular area, either labelled "Earthwork" as in Figure 2 or "Camp", on the Harmondsworth side of the Harmondsworth-Harlington parish boundary and about a quarter mile south of the Bath Road. The earliest reference to the site occurs in the map of Hundred of Isleworth* drawn by Moses Glover 1635. It is just beyond the boundary of Glover's map but near to the River Crane he records *"In this Heathe (i.e. Hounslow Heath) hath many camps bin pitched... whereof the forme of two yet in parte remayneth not far beyond this rive. By the name of Shakesbury Hilles"*. Rocque's map of Middlesex* published in 1764 (Figure 3) records the two camps, mentioned by Glover, under the names of Shasbury Hill and Fern Hill. By the time (1819) that the Harmonsworth Inclosure Map was published, Fern Hill had disappeared (for information on Fern Hill ses reference 5) and the other was recorded as Schapsbury Hill.

The appearance of the hill on all the maps indicates that it must have

*Reproductions of both of these maps have been published by Hounslow Borough Libraries

been particularly prominent in the otherwise flat terrain. The site was examined by Stukeley in 1723 who believed it to be a Roman encampment. He said it was nearly perfect and sixty paces square, but he did not say why he recognised it as a Roman site or why he called it "Caesar's Camp". Stukeley's drawing of the site is shown in Figure 4.

Lysons, writing at the end of the 18th century also mentions the earthwork, stating that it consisted of a single trench about three hundred feet square. After the Inclosure the earthwork was ploughed flat but was still significant enough for it to be marked on maps. The full significance of the site became apparent in 1944, when excavations prior to the construction of the main runway revealed that the earthwork contained about twelve hut sites and the remains of a temple dating from the period 500-300 B.C.. This important, indeed unique, site was destroyed and buried under the main runway.

GENERAL ROY AND KING'S ARBOUR

Two thousand years later Hounslow Heath was chosen by General Roy to establish a baseline of accurately known length as a prelude to an accurate trigonometrical survey of Great Britain. Roy chose the site, *"because of its vicinity to the capital and the Royal Observatory at Greenwich, its great extent and the extraordinary*

Fig 4. Caesar's Camp 1723

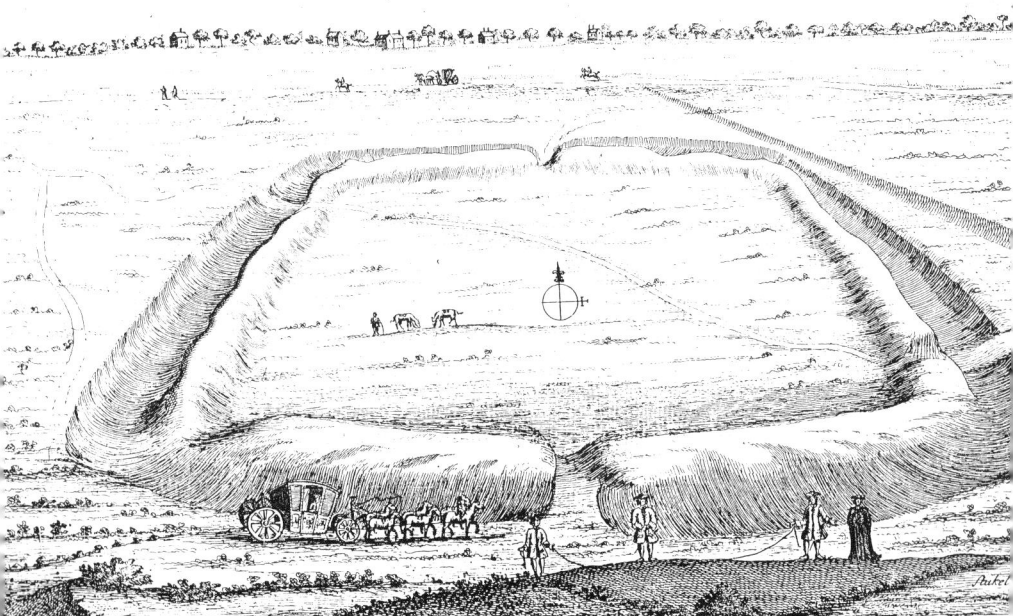

levelness of the surface without any local obstructions whatever to render the measurement difficult" (6). One end of his baseline was at King's Arbour, Heathrow, and the other at Hampton some five miles away.

According to Maxwell (Highwayman's Heath 7) *" King's Arbour got its name from the fact here was a stable used by George III who would not use inns for changing horses, but kept an establishment of his own"*. Maxwell had doubts about this alleged origin and in fact the name was in existence some 200 years before the reign of George III. A list of copyholders included in a survey of the land of Thomas Paget in 1587 (8) contains the following:

"Thomas Jackson and Joanna his wife hold a messuage with pertinances in Harmondsworth formerly held by William Rede paying per annum 2s 6d. The same hold two acres of land situate at King's Arbour called Otercroft paying per annum 2s 0d. The same hold a cottage in Heathrowe with two acres of land paying per annum 2s 0d."

As the name was well established in the reign of Queen Elizabeth this disposes of the myth that the name comes from King George having a stable there. The King referred to in the name was probably a member of the King family whose name occurs in records dating back as far as 1390 relating to Harmondsworth parish. Arbour may equate with the modern meaning of the word which came into English from the French. It can, however, have a much older origin derived from Old English *"earth-burh"* meaning earth fort. As King's Arbour was adjacent to the earthwork mentioned in the previous section it is quite possible that in this case the Arbour refers to the earthwork.

The association of King's Arbour with George III may originate from the fact that he was King at the time of Roy's survey and the small area of land around the end of the baseline was Crown property. The Harmondsworth Inclosure Award of 1819 records the King as the owner of this piece of land. It was only nine perches (30 square yards) in area and thus far too small to be used for stabling.

The exact location of the baseline was agreed on the ground by Roy accompanied by Sir Joseph Banks and Charles Blagden. The terminals were at King's Arbour and the Poor House at Hampton; soldiers were used to clear the ground between the two points and generally assist in the survey. The spire of a church, which Roy subsequently discovered was that of Banstead in Surrey, was found to be dead in line with the two ends of the base and provided a useful sighting point.

Rough measurement of the base, using a 100 ft. steel chain, started on 16 June 1784 and was completed by the end of the month. On 15 July precise measurements began using wooden (deal) rods but the weather was bad and it soon became apparent that, because of expansion and contraction of the wood with changes in humidity, wooden rods would not be sufficiently accurate. Glass tubes (referred to by Roy as rods) were suggested as a possible alternative by one of Roy's assistants and somewhat surprisingly were found to be suitable. It proved possible to obtain glass rods about 20 ft. in length and 1 inch in diameter and these rods were mounted in wooden cases. By using specially designed equipment for handling the rods measurements could be made along the length of the baseline. Work on this started on 17 August and was completed by the end of the month. An amusing aside was Roy's complaint that the carriages passing along the "Great Road" (the old Staines Road running from Hounslow to Staines) continually interrupted his work. The distance as measured by Roy was 27404.01 feet.

Roy marked the terminals of the baseline by wooden pipes and waggon wheels sunk into the ground. In 1791 these were found to be in an advanced state of decay and they were replaced by two cannon which had been condemned as unfit for further public service. They were half-buried in the ground muzzle upwards, one at each end of the baseline. In 1926 plaques commemorating the 200th anniversary of Roy's birth were fixed on top of both cannon. The inscription on that at King's Arbour is printed at the end of this section.

Because it was thought to be a potential danger to aircraft taxi-ing along a proposed runway, the cannon was removed in 1944 and stored at the Ordnance Survey temporary headquarters at Chessington. It has since been returned to its original position but the 1926 plaque is now mounted on a sloping concrete block on the south side of the cannon (Figure 5). The cannon at the southeast terminal of the baseline is now surrounded by a small housing estate known as "Roy Grove" at Hampton.

Inscription on the cannon at King's Arbour

THIS TABLET WAS / AFFIXED IN 1926 TO COMMEMORATE / THE 200th ANNIVERSARY OF THE BIRTH OF / MAJOR-GENERAL WILLIAM ROY F.R.S. / BORN 4th MAY 1726 DIED 1st JULY 1790 / HE CONCEIVED THE IDEA OF CARRYING OUT THE TRIANGULATION / OF THIS COUNTRY AND OF CONSTRUCTING A COMPLETE AND / ACCURATE MAP AND THEREBY LAID THE FOUNDATION OF / THE ORDNANCE SURVEY THIS GUN MARKS THE N.W. TERMINAL OF THE BASE WHICH WAS MEASURED IN 1784 / UNDER THE SUPERVISION OF GENERAL ROY AS PART OF THE OPERATIONS FOR / DETERMINING THE RELATIVE POSITION OF THE GREENWICH AND PARIS / OBSERVATORIES - THIS MEASUREMENT / WAS RENDERED POSSIBLE BY THE / MUNIFICENCE OF H.M. KING GEORGE III WHO INSPECTED THE WORK ON 21st AUGUST 1784. / THIS BASE WAS MEASURED AGAIN IN 1791 BY CAPTAIN MUDGE AS THE COMMENCEMENT / OF THE PRINCIPAL TRIANGULATION OF GREAT BRITAIN. / LENGTH OF BASE - REDUCED TO M.S.L.

AS MEASURED BY ROY   27404.01 FEET
AS MEASURED BY MUDGE   27404.24 FEET
AS DETERMINED BY CLARKE IN TERMS
OF THE ORDNANCE SURVEY STANDARD 27406.19 FEET

THE HAMLET OF HEATHROW

Heathrow appears to have been the last of the settlements to be formed in Harmondsworth Parish. Harmondsworth itself is in the north-west of the parish and the name is first mentioned in an Anglo-Saxon charter of 780 AD, when land in a place called Hermonds was granted by Offa, King of Mercia to his servant Aeldred. By the time of Domesday the name had become Hermondesworde. Sipson, now the second largest settlement in the parish, is first referred to in 1214 when it was known as Sibbeston, Longford is first mentioned in 1337 and the first known reference to Heathrow is in 1453. All the names are of Anglo-Saxon origin and in all cases must have existed long before the first recorded references.

Fig 5. NW Terminal of General Roy's baseline

The settlement of Heathrow was spread out in a straggling manner on the west side of Heathrow Road from the Bath Road to Perry Oaks (see Figure 2). Perry Oaks itself could almost be regarded as separate from Heathrow and it had direct access from the Bath Road via Tithe Barn Lane. The area bounded by Heathrow Road, Tithe Barn Lane and the Bath Road was before the Inclosure of Harmondsworth Parish in 1819 one of the open fields of the parish and was known as Heathrow Field. The area to the south and east of Heathrow Road was the common land of the parish and formed the western edge of Hounslow Heath. Heathrow as its name suggests was on the edge of the Heath bordered by the open arable fields of Harmondsworth Parish (Figure 3). It was not in the centre of a blasted uninhabited heath, as the aviation lobby is apt to suggest when seeking justification for its destruction to make way for the airport.

Before the Inclosure the use of the Common by the parishioners was governed by rules some of which are recorded in the presentments of the Homages of the Court Baron held for the Manor of Harmondsworth on the 23 July 1778. These record that:

"none of the inhabitants (of the parish) shall put upon the Common belonging to this parish any sheep before the fourth day of July and no more than six sheep to a family and to continue there no longer than the nineteenth day of September following on the penalty of five shillings per head. Also we find and present that no one who is not a parishioner nor inmate shall put or keep any cattle upon the Common belonging to this parish on the penalty of five shillings per head for any that shall be kept contrary to this order".

Although the Common was enclosed in 1819 the name persisted and the area was still referred to as such by older people in the parish until the final obliteration in 1944. After the Inclosure the opportunity existed to up-grade the quality of the land and, despite the proximity to Hounslow Heath with its notorious connotations of sterility, the whole area developed into high quality agricultural land in a manner that would have astonished Cobbett.

AGRICULTURE

Before it was overwhelmed by the airport West Middlesex had been an important market gardening area with Heathrow itself virtually in the centre of what remained of the Thames Valley Market Gardening Plain (see References 9 & 10 and Figure 6).

The reason for this was that the brickearth soils of the Heathrow area by virtue of their texture, topography and drainage were ideally suited to intensive agriculture. Moreover, the inherent fertility of the soils had been greatly improved over the years by the addition of huge quantities of horse manure arising from the immense horse population of London. (Until well into this century all the traffic in London was horse-drawn. The disposal of the horse-droppings would have been a serious problem had it not been for the fact that the market gardening wagons trundling into London each day with fresh fruit and vegetables were able to make the return journey loaded with manure).

The report of the Land Utilisation Survey in 1935 (10) lamented the fact that, *"at least four aerodromes have been recently established in the region three of them involving the conversion of excellent market-gardening land into grassland of little agricultural value"*. The three aerodromes referred to must have been Heston,

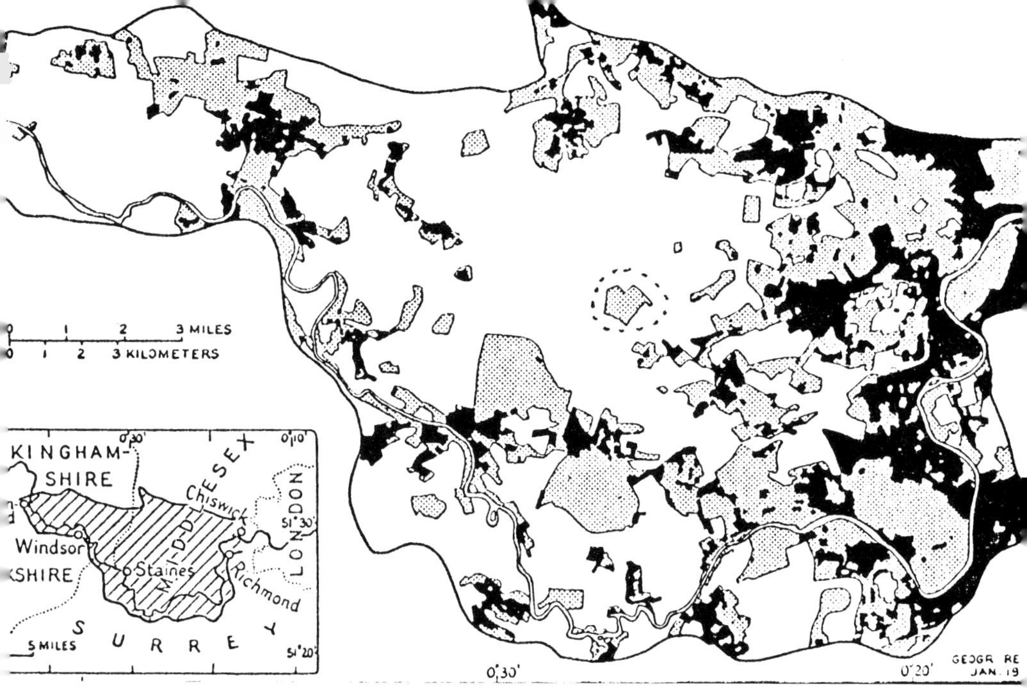

Fig 6. The Thames Valley Market Garden Plain 1936.
The solid line delineates the area of the first class arable soil which constituted the region. The areas in non-agricultural use in 1914 are show in black. The strippled areas are those that passed out of agricultural use between 1914 and 1936. The Fairey airfield in the centre of the map has been circled by a dotted line

Fairey's at Heathrow and Hawker's at Langley. These are among the areas shown in stipple in Figure 6 (reproduced from the LUS report) which denotes the areas lost to agriculture between 1914 and 1936; on this map the Fairey airfield has been circled by a dotted line.

Fig 7. Ploughing Match, Tithe Barn Lane, Heathrow 1935

The loss of land to the airfield had little effect on the rural nature of the area and it can be seen, from Figures 1 and 6, that the Heathrow area represented the last significant tract of Grade 1 agricultural land in West Middlesex still in use for intensive production at the outbreak of war in 1939.

This meant that the Heathrow area was the natural choice for staging the annual ploughing matches organised by the Middlesex Agricultural and Growers' Association (Figure 7). These were held in early autumn directly after the harvest. The last match ever to be held was the ninety-ninth which took place on 28 September 1937 on the farm of J.E.Philp and Son of Heathrow Hall on land in Tithe Barn Lane, Heathrow. The 100th match which would have been held in 1938 was postponed because of the desire of the government to avoid large gatherings at the time of the Munich crisis. The outbreak of war one year later meant that it never took place as the matches were not resumed at the end of hostilities largely because most of the suitable sites had by then been buried under concrete.

OTHER INDUSTRY

The Perry Oaks Sludge Works.

A short distance past Perry Oaks Farm on the western side of what was Tithe Barn Lane was (and still is) the Perry Oaks sludge disposal works. These works which now occupy an enclave of some 250 acres on the western edge of the airport were opened by the Middlesex County Council in 1935 as part of the West Middlesex Main Drainage Scheme. The main sewage works is at Mogden, Isleworth, where sludge is separated from the sewage and, after initial treatment at Mogden, is pumped over a seven mile distance to Perry Oaks. The sludge is pumped through a 12-inch cast iron main which follows the route of the Bath Road and the former route of Tithe Barn Lane. Had the route chosen followed a more direct line by going across the fields to Perry Oaks it is quite probable that it would have rendered the construction of the airport too difficult to achieve. In any event the presence of the sludge works has proved to be a thorn in the side of the aviation authorities and, as will be seen later, they have been trying with little success for the past 45 years to relocate the sludge works.

Gravel digging.

As mentioned in the section on topography, gravel underlies the topsoil throughout much of the Thames Valley and the harmful effects of gravel extraction have always been a cause for concern. Figure 6 shows the land in the Thames Market Gardening Plain lost to agriculture between 1914 and 1936 much of which was due to gravel digging. The area around Feltham had been devastated by gravel digging in the early 1930's and later in the decade gravel working had extended to Heathrow. The area of the workings was confined to the east side of Heathrow Road and by the time the airport was developed in 1944 an area of about 200 acres had been excavated. As the water table is high the excavations soon filled with water which did something to ameliorate the effects.

THE FAIREY AERODROME

Aviation at Heathrow started in 1929 with the purchase by the Fairey Aviation Company of 150 acres of land in Cain's Lane. Here they laid out an area of high quality turf to construct an airfield which was used for the first time in the late summer of 1930. It was known initially as the "Harmondsworth Aerodrome"

FLYING PROGRAMME

May 14th, 1939
at

THE FAIREY AVIATION COMPANY'S AERODROME
(The Great West Aerodrome, near Hayes)

(By kind permission of Mr. C. R. Fairey, M.B.E., F.R.Ae.S.)

The following is an outline of the arrangements. They are subject to such alterations as may be found necessary at the time. Any change will be announced on the loud speakers.

It is particularly requested, in order that arrangements may run as smoothly as possible, that members and their guests will vacate their seats in the marquees as soon as they have had their teas.

p.m.
2.30—3.0   Reception by the President, Mr. A. H. R. Fedden, D.Sc., M.B.E., F.R.Ae.S.
(The reception is at the reception tent near the flagstaff and hangars)

Time	Firm	Pilot	Aircraft	Engine
14.50-14.58	Reid and Sigrist	G. Lowdell	Twin-engined Trainer	2 Gipsy Sixes
15.00-15.08	Vickers Aviation, Ltd.	J. Summers	Wellington	Pegasus XVIII's
15.10-15.18	Blackburn Aircraft, Ltd.	Flt.-Lt. Bailey	Skua	Perseus XII
15.20-15.28	Percival Aircraft, Ltd.	Cpt. Percival	Q.6	2 Gipsy Sixes
		D. M. Bray	Mew Gull	Gipsy VI
15.30-15.38	General Aircraft, Ltd.	D. Hollis-Williams	Cygnet, with tricycle under-carriage	
15.40-15.48	Boulton Paul Aircraft	C. Feather	Defiant	Merlin
15.50-15.58	Fairey Aviation Co.	F. H. Dixon	P4/34	Merlin Rm2M
16.00-16.08	Cierva Autogiro Co.	R. A. C. Brie	Type C40	Salmson 9Nd
16.10-16.38		TEA INTERVAL.		
	During the tea interval there will be a demonstration at 16.10-16.24 by 9 Supermarine Spitfires of No. 74 Fighter Squadron, and at 16.26-16.38 a demonstration by 9 Bristol Blenheims of No. 601 Fighter Squadron of the Auxiliary Air Force.			
16.40-16.48	The Willoughby Delta Co.	Capt. A. M. Kingwill	Willoughby St. Francis	2 Menasco Pirate C4
		S. Appleby	Schelde Musch	Praga B

Fig 8. Flying Programme of Royal Aeronautical Society 1939

but later as the "Great West Aerodrome". It was renowned for its level and smooth turf and the hangar sited on the northern corner of the site was said at one time to be the largest in the world, although this seems hard to believe.

The airfield was purchased as a result of the Company having been given notice by the Air Ministry to vacate leased premises at Northolt which the company used for flight testing. Fairey's had carried out flight tests from Northolt since 1917, the airfield being placed conveniently to their factory in North Hyde Road, Hayes. The Heathrow site proved just as convenient and had the advantage that the company held the freehold - little did they know that the Air Ministry having expelled them from Northolt would eventually compulsorily acquire their new site at Heathrow! Because of the obvious advantages the company decided to expand the site so that it could transfer the factory from Hayes to Heathrow thus bringing the works and flight testing facilities together. With this end in view Fairey's gradually acquired additional land, as opportunity occurred, and by 1943 they owned about 200 acres of land between Cain's Lane, High Tree Lane and the Duke of Northumberland's river.

The presence of the airfield did little to disturb the rural scene; it had no concrete runways, few buildings and only a small number of test flights. The airfield was, in fact, quite a local attraction as it was a novelty then to see aeroplanes at such close quarters. From 1935-1939 the aerodrome was the venue for the garden party of the Royal Aeronautical Society (The front page of the programme of the last ever garden party to be held at Heathrow is reproduced in Figure 8). At these parties a wide variety of aircraft were gathered from light planes to gliders, from military aircraft to new civil airliners fresh from the production lines. There were also numerous aeronautical displays so that during the one day of the party more people visited Heathrow than the total for the rest of the year.

NORTHERN HEIGHTS
MODEL FLYING CLUB
(Affiliated to The Society of Model Aeronautical Engineers).

SIXTH

Annual Gala Meeting

Full Programme of Events

SUNDAY, JUNE 19th, 1938
11 a.m. until dusk.

The Great West Aerodrome

HEATHROW, MIDDLESEX. (near Great West Rd.)
(For directions see Page No. 1).

Fig 9. Annual Gala meeting of the Model Flying Club 1937

The Fairey Aviation Company had been founded in 1915 by (Charles) Richard Fairey (1887-1956). In his youth Fairey had been a model aeroplane enthusiast and he retained a life-long interest in model aircraft. This interest made him sympathetic to the requests of model aeroplane clubs to use his aerodrome at weekends when it was not being used for any other purposes. The aerodrome was the regular Sunday venue for members of the Hayes Model Aeroplane Club who flew their models at Heathrow, and it was also used by other clubs which often travelled long distances to use the aerodrome (see Figure 9). One of the hazards for the model flying clubs was the Duke of Northumberland's river which formed the southern boundary of the airfield (Figure 13).

The Fairey aerodrome and the large number of people in the aviation world who visited it at the time of the Garden Parties were undoubtedly what led the aviation interests to cast covetous eyes on Heathrow as a site for a civil airport for London. However, if war had not broken out in 1939 it would have proved impossible for them to acquire Fairey's airfield and the surrounding land. As will be described in Part 2, the war presented the opportunity for the whole area to be requisitioned and to begin the development of a civil airport under the pretext that it was needed as a base for the RAF.

A WALK ROUND HEATHROW IN 1935

by
DAVID WILD

Author's Note: This section is taken from an unpublished manuscript of the "History of Harmondsworth Parish" written by the late Mr.David Wild who, with his brother John, owned a farm in Cain's Lane, Heathrow until they were evicted to make way for the airport in 1944. It replaces a section written by me based on my own recollections of Heathrow gained largely when as a schoolboy I worked on Mr. Wild's farm in my summer holidays during the early years of the war. Mr Wild's account is much more comprehensive and interesting than mine and has therefore been included by kind permission of his son Mr. William Wild who was born at the farm in Cain's Lane and lived there until he was eight and a half. It recalls a pastoral scene described by Gordon Maxwell in "Highwayman's Heath (7) as follows:

"*If you turn down from the Bath Road by the "Three Magpies" you will come upon a road that is as rural as anywhere in England. It is not, perhaps, scenically wonderful but for detachment from London or any urban interests it would be hard to find its equal; there is a calmness and serenity about it that is soothing in a mad rushing world*".

Fig 10. The "Three Magpies", Bath Road 1988. The last surving coaching inn on the Bath Road at

All the hamlet's houses were in the lane beside the "Three Magpies" (Figure 10). First came the row of Doghurst Cottages, named after a large house known as Doghurst which stood north of the Bath Road and to the east of Sipson House - it was pulled down before my time. The owner of Doghurst must have been a public-spirited man for beyond Doghurst Cottages there was a hall which he had built for the recreation of the lads of the village. In my earliest memory the hall was used by the Staines Rural District Council. Mr.Flood the Harmondsworth Rate Collector used it as his office. At the rear of the hall was a mortuary chiefly used for deaths in road accidents.

The cannon at King's Arbour stood in Mr. Patrick Howell's fruit garden with an iron fence around it. He told me that the land inside the fence was not his but he could use it rent-free; so his rhubarb under the trees was both inside and outside the fence. Adjoining the field containing the cannon and right on the road were Mr Howell's farm buildings with his house known as "Bathurst" just beyond. Opposite "Bathurst" was one of the fruit gardens of W & S Philp with neat rows of paeonies and bulbs. Beside these were two modern villas in one of which lived Mr. Ward the Harmondsworth Headmaster. Mr. Forse and later Mr. Knapp the Sipson school heads lived in the School House adjoining the school, opposite the "Old Magpies".

Beyond Messrs Philp's market garden across a meadow was an attractive old thatched house where lived the two west-country families of the Biddescombes. It was always a pleasure to meet these kindly little men, if only to listen to the sound of their Somerset burr. Then we came to Heathrow Hall (Figure 11) still on the right-hand side of the road, with its wide sweeping Cedar of Lebanon on the lawn close to the house and a pond on the opposite side of the road. Beyond the house the large stackyard enclosed on three sides by tall Dutch Barns,

Fig 11. Heathrow Hall 1935

THE HISTORY OF HEATHROW

having ample space within, at threshing time, for both steam engine and drum. Also a nice sheltered spot for lambing pens. This homestead I look on as where Heathrow began.

And so to Heathrow our last Middlesex home. Starting at Heathrow Hall all the old homesteads lay on the right-hand side of the road. After the Hall's buildings was a small meadow and then Palmer's Farm with its back door opening directly into the farm yard. Then a group of modern cottages opposite and beyond Wheatcut or Wheatcut Corner - this was its local name, I have seen it nowhere in print. At this corner Heathrow Road curved sharply to the right with Perrott's Farm laying off the road behind a small meadow. Although everyone called it Perrott's Farm it was owned for many years by the Parrott family. The last of them, John Parrott, married Rebecca Weekley. His body lies on the south side of Harmondsworth Church with his little son John Weekley Parrott who died as a boy, so sadly the name is gone from the parish. Martha Parrott owned the farm at the time of the Inclosure (1816); the farm was larger then for this lady owned land on both sides of the road and at Wheatcut Corner. The land on the south side of the road then passed to the Tilliers who doubtless planted the fruit trees. Then W & S Philp of Harlington underplanted it with paeonies and bulbs. Finally in 1938, just at the time of the Munich crisis, my brother and I took it over and grubbed up the trees. The land here was far and away the best that we occupied during the war. Glad we were of such to add to our limited acreage when cropping had to change from flowers to mainly vegetables.

Running out from Heathrow Road were three lanes on to the Heath. The first of these started at Wheatcut Corner, this branch was Cain's Lane (* see footnote) exactly one mile in length and straight as an arrow through the middle of the pre-inclosure Common. All I know of the Common was the part we held, doubtless the rest was the same and laid out in the old measurements of chains, furlongs and miles.

We gave our new home the name of Croft House when it was built in 1927 but right up to the time we left in 1944 we received letters simply addressed to "The Common, Heathrow". Our postman also lived on the Common, he delivered by motor bicycle from Hounslow with the mail on two panniers over his rear wheel. Ours was his last call before his breakfast in Common Barn opposite. those lower down the road received post from Feltham - which Post Office later took on responsibility for our thin population for a while. After that two more changes, but to our old friends in Longford we were just "up at the Common".

The two oldest houses in Cain's Lane were about half-way along it. On the left an ancient boarded dwelling named Heathrow House, where lived Mrs Place with her black and white English Setter always at her heels. The name of her house was confusing, being a half-mile beyond Heathrow - a trifle irritating for her when her letters addressed thus arrived a day late. Cain's Farm House was nearly opposite; according to my ancestor Richard Weekley's diary on 14 February 1834 Mr Cain's premises were all burnt down So all that remained of the lovely old house and an adjacent pair of cottages were the few small farm buildings adjoining Mr.Cryer's modern piggery. When he retired the Watkinson brothers from Two

---

* *On the left of Cain's Lane were two modern farmhouses (Figure 12) belonging respectively to David Wild and his brother John whose family had farmed in the parish for more than three hundred years. On a corner of their farm and adjoining the road was a corrugated iron mission hall which had been erected in 1901. This belonged to the Baptist church at Sipson and was the only "church" in Heathrow, although there had been earlier churches at Heathrow belonging to non-conformist sects.*

Fig 12. *Modern Farmhouses at Heathrow 1944*

Bridges Farm on the Harmondsworth boundary at Bedfont took over the land.

In medieval days there was free pannage for pigs in the forest of Harmondsworth, adjoining the Common over which after harvest the pigs could roam and glean the corn. Right up to the last the Common still had many pigs. During the war we fattened a few in the buildings at Common Barn, augmenting their rations with surplus tulip bulbs and later Tottenham pudding from the Waste Food Products Co. at West Bedfont. A far larger pig producer on the Common was Mr. John Heyward who had them running in his orchards. Mr. Curtis kept a large number in the buildings of Perrott's Farm, and at the other end of Heathrow, Mrs Sherwood had a small up-to-date pig farm.

Middlesex has always had more pigs per acre of agricultural land than any other county, London being so close. The wasteful eating habits of so many who live there provides an economical source of food for the pigs. Country folk who grow food never waste it, but are only too happy to glean for their pigs any crumbs that fall from the townsman's table.

One colourful personality we had riding down Cain's Lane was the barber cum cycle-repairer who had his little shop in Faggs Road at Hatton Cross. Each Saturday afternoon he came along perched on his penny-farthing bicycle, with leather case to hold his shaving outfit slung bandolier-fashion across his back. He was going to visit men too elderly or infirm to visit him.

To continue round Heathrow, after the small meadow in front of Perrott's Farm was the "Plough and Harrow" Beer House with Mr. Basham, an ex-policeman and so most suitable, as landlord. Exactly opposite the "Plough and Harrow" stood the neat ivy-clad house and small fruit and flower-holding of old John Dance and his wife. Much of the bulb and other flower-growing of Harmondsworth parish was on its lighter land. About 100 years ago my grandfather had several acres of the old double Van Sion daffodil, Most of these he grew up at the Common, the flowers were sold at Covent Garden. Every second year the bulbs were ploughed out and the largest of them sold. The chief customer was the noted firm of Seed and Bulb Merchants, Watkins and Simpson of Feltham.

Beyond the "Plough and Harrow" was the market garden of George Dance and Sons. Their holding, which was larger than John's, grew vegetables. After this Heathrow Farm with its picturesque old house surrounded by a low wall in a rear corner of the farmyard. Here following his father in the same farm lived Harry Curtis. Harry and I were in the same form at Ashford County School for a little while, so he was about my age. He grew both corn and vegetables and grew them well. Just beyond Heathrow Farm and on the left started the second of those roads out of Heathrow across the Heath where High Tree Lane branched off to the left.

It was called High Tree Lane,* from the tall elm trees behind a pond at its start. From Two Bridges Farm at Bedfont to Old Oak Common the Duke's (of Northumberland) River formed the south-eastern boundary of Harmondsworth parish so this second lane ended (for our parish) at Goat House Tree Ford, where to cross the river was a footbridge (* see footnote). It continued as Goathouse Tree Lane to cross the Longford River at West Bedfont. Late one evening during the Battle of Britain, I was by this ford and spotted a few Hurricane fighters hidden near the very high hedge by the river in the south-west corner of Fairey's flying ground. Sometimes at dusk the machines were far from their base and landed at any convenient airfield. When they did so here, some of the housewives in our part of Heathrow had the privilege of providing a bed for them. My mother kept one for this purpose and two or three times, much to her delight, it was used.

I shall never forget one evening at dusk standing with her and one of those pilots outside her back door. North-east of us was Southall Gasometer lit up by a huge fire behind it. Sadly the young man said, "I know by that gasholder that the fire is in London's docks". Later we heard he was correct.

After High Tree Lane we reach the centre of our scattered hamlet and its only shop kept by Mr. Field, a sufferer from tuberculosis. He should have lived in a more bracing climate than ours. Here clustered around a tiny green were five or six dwellings. The best a Tudor timber-framed thatched farmhouse (Figure 14) half of which was occupied by Miss Harbour and her companion Miss Hickmott. For many years these two valiantly supported Heathrow Mission Hall along with Mr and Mrs Best who lived in Cain's Lane. Harbour is a long-standing name in Heathrow. It may be that our old friend's ancestors farmed from this house - perhaps using the buildings opposite. Here also lived several families of the Lipscombes, another old name. Adjoining this group was a row of cottages facing the road, one of which was the shop.

---

*High Tree Lane was another of the Inclosure Commissioner's roads, it ran in a straight line to West Bedfont. Half a mile along High Tree Lane at a ford marked on maps as "Goathouse Tree Ford" the road crossed the Duke of Northumberland's river. This is man-made, the channel having been constructed in the mid 16th-century to increase the water driving Isleworth Mill and to provide water to Syon House. It runs from the Colne at West Drayton by way of Longford, Heathrow and Bedfont to join the Crane for a short distance at Baber Bridge before proceeding on its own course to Isleworth. (The origins of the river are rather obscure, for a discussion of these see Reference 11) When construction of the airport began in 1944 it was diverted to a more southerly route for about two miles of its length but the route of its former channel still forms the southern boundary of Harmondsworth parish and hence of the Borough of Hillingdon.
Goathouse Tree Ford was seldom, if ever, referred to as such and the area of the ford was known locally as High Tree River. It was a local beauty spot popular for picnics where children could safely paddle in the water and fish for "tiddlers". Although the very occasional traffic had to use the ford, there was a footbridge high above the river, (which had rather high banks probably as a result of the deposition of spoil during its construction - Figure 13). The banks were well- wooded and on the south side was a riverside walk to Longford about two miles away.

Fig 13. Duke of Northumberland's River 1937. (The river was a hazard to model aeroplane enthusiasts using the Fairey airfield!)

Fig 14. Cottages at Heathrow 1935

About 150 yards beyond these was another old house standing nearby an acre of ground. It was well-cropped with fruit and vegetables except for the part occupied by a range of pig-sties surrounding which were heaps of various agricultural deadstock. Mr. Burton who lived here was quite a character. In my time he was an old man, but I gather that in his younger days he carried on a successful marine store business, visiting local markets, auction sales etc. Beside his garden started Pease Path almost straight, three quarters of a mile long and four feet wide. This led to the Bath Road at Pumpshire Gap almost opposite where the Technicolor factory now stands. Beyond Mr. Burtons were relatively modern houses and buildings at intervals on both sides of the road until we come to the three-way junction at Heathrow's far end where stood Perry Oaks Farm. Here branched to the left the third of the lanes into the Heath, across Old Oak common with bridges over the same two rivers as the last (High Tree Lane) to the "Rising Sun" in Stanwell.

Perry Oaks Farm (Figure 15) was the most beautifully situated homestead in all our parish and nearly all of the farm good land. For most of this century's first half this large fruit farm was occupied by Mr. Sidney Whittington. For a considerable part of the 19th century occupied as arable by Richard Weekley and after him his cousin Henry. Richard's lease was dated 18 March 1800 with most strict conditions:

Fig 15 Perry Oaks Farm 1937

"Not to plow up any meadow or pasture, or by any other means destroy the sward under penalty of £30 per acre. Manure enclosed meadow and lands every third year and not take therefrom more than one crop of hay yearly. In each year one third of the arable in fallow, clover or turnips. Shall not take two crops of white corn successively from any of the enclosed lands but shall introduce an ameliorating crop between. Shall manure the premises with dung arising from the hay and straw grown, or by two loads of dung for every load of hay or straw carried away. Shall leave the Dove House stocked with thirty dozen of pigeons at the end of the term."

No ranch-farming permitted when England was engaged in a life and death struggle with the would-be world dictator Napoleon!

The continuation of Heathrow round Perry Oaks corner was Bragg's Way (also known as Tithe Barn Lane). Here to complete the semi-circle of fertile land enclosed by the Bath Road, Heathrow Road and the Duke's River we must cross the lane to include the best part of Perry Oaks land which extended almost to Longford. Beyond on the farm's north-west boundary was Broad Platt and north of that, up to the Bath Road - Fairview Farm. West of this Long Breakfast along the bank of the river. So we come to the end of our fertile semi-circle at the Colne's many-streamed delta.

I have described the farms that lie round Heathrow's edge. What of the vast amount of land behind intersected by Pease Path as well as the large fields in front of Heathrow Hall Farmhouse stretching to the parish boundary near Harlington Police station?. All this at the Inclosure was awarded to George Bing Esq., a large part of it "in lieu of Tithe". Hence no tithe has had to be paid in Harmondsworth since then. I take it that George Bing was an ancestor of the Earl of Strafford of Wrotham Park, Potter's Bar who eventually sold the land to his tenant Josiah Philp, whose eldest son Fred lived at Heathrow Hall. Bragg's Way which ran from Perry Oaks corner to Shepherd's Pool on the Bath Road was later named Tithe Barn Lane from the barn half-way along on the western side (* see footnote). My guess is that Geo. Bing or an ancestor in about 1774 had part of the Harmondsworth Tithe Barn moved as he needed it as much as the Lords of the Manor (the Paget family). What a pity it was, as the moved part lasted just 100 years. The Bucks Advertiser reported on February 2 1874 that this barn was blown down in a gale when, "Oak beams as thick as a man's body were splintered like matchwood". All I knew were the low walls on the foundations at the west side of the lane about two furlongs south of Shepherd's Pool - a delightful spot on the Bath Road.

This Pool, as several other large and small roadside ponds, was dug for gravel to mend the roads. Doubtless this one obtained its name as drovers would rest their flocks here on the long journey from the west country to London markets. The Pool surrounded by a fair amount of grass must have made an ideal spot to rest under the shade of willows on a hot summer's day or even for the night. A similar pond with grass surround covering two acres was in Heathrow opposite Palmer's Farm. A pair of swans nested on the pond every year. Behind it camped two Romany families for most of the year apart from "hopping time" when some of the waggons moved south.

---

*The barn is said to have been a wing of the Tithe Barn at Harmondsworth which had been dismantled and re-erected. There is no real evidence for this as a detailed examination of the inside and outside stucture of the existing Tithe Barn shows no indication that it ever had an additional wing. However, Mr Wild's account agrees with many others on this subject.

LAMENT FOR HEATHROW 1944

We shall remember thee in days to come
Before the ruthless hand of man had spoiled
When sweet peace lingered on thy country brow,
The day when sound of plover lulled thee,
The night when screech owl loved thy lonely shade
We shall remember thee, although the time
Of visitation great had come!
No longer is there peace within thy gates
That peace which was thy birthright. Now they come
They strip the wealth and riches from the soil
Although most fertile land in all the south,
But now the tyrant's hand hath claimed thee,
Cruel progress would not pass unheeding by.
Soon will be nought to mark thy borders trim-
No hedge, no tree, no wayside flowerets fair-
Naught that is lovely left. Oh woe the day!
Long years have passed since Rome raised camp on thee,
And yet they passed, and left thee undisturbed
Hadst thou a voice couldst tell us of this past,
But now men want to rob of all thy grace
Full comely thou dost seem as we must go
And so "Goodbye" - a long a last farewell.
For some short while the larks may still come home-
The weasel, mole and fieldmouse tunnel round;
Yet as the circling days go swiftly by
Soon will be gone all traces of the past
Save in our memories fond - we'll still
Remember Heathrow.

John Wild 1944

● ●

With the exception of our few Common neighbours these Romanies were about our nearest, just one field lay between us. Some of the women worked for us through the years, usually bunching. The artistic fingers of Sarah and Lavinia Smith and Betty and Trainee (?) Loveridge were the most skilled we had. Flower-bunching is a real Romany art. Of the young men a few came hoeing, I recall Bert Smith and William Loveridge. Also Wisdom Smith an older man; he once told me that Gipsy Smith, the celebrated evangelist, was his cousin. Several years earlier I heard this cousin address a large audience in the Albert Hall. The Rev. R. Ross our vicar arranged for a party to go from Harmondsworth. In graphic words "Gipsy" told the story of his father's conversion. In early life his father had been a wife-beater and drunkard of whom his young children lived in terror. But one day Christ entered that tent, even their dog knew that something had happened. It was not long before the aim of every young Romany was realised and he had a waggon of his own. No wonder Wisdom felt proud to claim relationship.

Before leaving Heathrow mention should be made of our blacksmith Oliver Newell one of, if not, the best in the south of England. The awards mentioned on his billheads showed his prowess at shoeing. He was a craftsman capable of any skilled work in iron, following his father in the same forge in the Hatton Road just outside our parish boundary. He kept on his window-sill a few pairs of the stirrups and shoes he remembered his father making. Heathrow as well as Hatton farmers took their work to him. Many a tool both large and small he made for us, and when it came to dismantling the place in 1944 his jemmy and large pincers were better shaped and forged than any you can buy now.

Finally I must pay tribute to those who in the war-years were the most willing workers we had. The Women's Land Army. With the opening of hostilities the Romany population disappeared. At last we turned to Land Girls and found them to be the same breed as our father had at Longford in the Great War.

We were sad at having to leave Heathrow, and the poem written by my brother at the time, which appeared in the Uxbridge local paper describes how many of us felt. But now looking back I am inclined to think that our undisturbed neighbours trying to produce food from the few acres of the fertile plain still left to them are the more to be pitied.

POSTSCRIPT

A third of the 28 buildings in Harmondsworth parish listed by the Royal Commission on Historic Monuments in 1935 (12) were in Heathrow - by far the smallest of the four villages in the parish. The fact that Heathrow Hall (Figure 11) was not included in this list illustrates the high standard set by the RCHM which hardly corresponds with the description of the houses as, *"wretched little huts of weatherboard and thatch"* given in a recent book about Heathrow (13). Some of the buildings are illustrated in Figures 10 - 15 and are described in David Wild's account. What the photographs and the account do not reveal is the appearance of the hedgerows and verges which also added much to the rural scene. A description by Tony Harman of the hedgerows of Buckinghamshire in the 1920's and 1930's published in "The Guardian" (June 29 1989) could well have been written of Heathrow:

"Early in the spring big white patches of blackthorn appeared, associated in people's minds with a cold snap, the so-called blackthorn winter; a false assumption though. Soon after came the may on the hawthorn trees. Not long after the last hawthorn petals had fallen, the hedges were festooned with honeysuckle and that lasted a long time, overlapping the season where there were wild roses everywhere, some pink some white.

As soon as the roses had gone, bramble flowers were hanging off the branches. By September there were big dark purplish-blue sloes where the blackthorn had been, and blackberries where the bramble flowers were. And everywhere else red berries on the May trees (haws - but known as agars to the children of the Heathrow area); big bright red berries where the roses had been (hips); and round, red berries of innumerable plants one had hardly noticed before.

Over it all were great drifts of what looked almost like human hair - Old Man's Beard. Its flowers had been green and inconspicuous, but you notice it in the winter all right, big strands and tresses of it."

Tony Harman does not mention the verges but at Heathrow there was a drainage ditch under the hedge and then a wide verge, both of which were rich in wild flowers such as red and white campion, ragged robin, harebells, ox-eye daisies, with willow herb and yellow iris beside the ponds.

What also fails to come over in David Wild's account is the general quietness of the area. Elsewhere in his manuscript he mentions that the bells of the churches at Harmondsworth (1 mile away) and Stanwell (2 miles away) could be heard in Longford. He says that to hear the bells of Harmondsworth in Longford was a sign of fine weather but that if the bells of Stanwell could be heard this meant wet weather. I can remember, as a child, being able to tell the time by the chime of the church clock at Harlington which was over 1 mile from my home. Now although I live within sight of the church, only 200 yards away, it is sometimes difficult to hear the clock strike above the noise of aircraft and the constant roar of the traffic.

PART 2

THE DEVELOPMENT OF THE AIRPORT 1943 - 1951

THE ORIGINS OF THE DEVELOPMENT

Before the war, civil aviation interests in Great Britain were overseen by the Air Ministry. The Ministry was frequently subjected to severe criticism because of its alleged lack of interest in civil aviation matters. However, unbeknown to the critics, there was within the Ministry a faction that was fanatically devoted to civil aviation and, as events would show, would go to extraordinary lengths to further its interests. The idea of constructing a civil airport at Heathrow must have been first discussed among those responsible within the Air Ministry as early as 1942. This was at a time when the outcome of the war was by no means certain and when everything was supposed to be subordinated to the war effort.

The first recorded mention of the proposals in the Air Ministry files, now deposited in the Public Record Office, is in mid 1943 (see Reference 14). It is clear from these that right from the start the development was envisaged as being for civil aviation. The proposal for its development as a Royal Air Force base was merely a ruse to circumvent a public inquiry and to quell criticism that the war effort was being diverted to matters that could await the end of hostilities.

Although many thought at the time that the primary, if not the only, purpose of the development of the airport was for civil aviation, the pretence that it was developed in response to the urgent need for a military airfield close to London is still officially maintained; even now most accounts give this as the reason for the development. It was not until 1973 in the autobiography (15) of Harold Balfour (later Lord Balfour of Inchrye) that the truth was finally admitted. Balfour was the Parliamentary Under Secretary of State for Air between 1938 and 1944 and in his autobiography he makes the astonishing claim:

"Almost the last thing I did in the Air Ministry of any importance was to hijack for Civil Aviation the land on which London Airport stands under the noses of resistant Ministerial colleagues. If hi-jack is too strong a term I plead guilty to the lesser crime of deceiving a cabinet Committee. Within the Department those of us who had studied postwar civil aviation needs knew that spreading out from the Fairey Aviation Company's small grass aerodrome on the Great West Staines Road was land ideal for London's main airport. We also knew that any thought of trying to get the land for civil aviation would have to go through complicated civil procedures and was bound to be resisted by Agriculture and Housing and maybe more Ministries. Therefore our only hope lay in taking over the Fairey field and adjacent land under wartime powers and regulations. These powers were drastic and positive and should not be employed for anything but war purposes.

"By now with German defeat only a matter of time, Senior Staffs were planning Phase Two of the war which was to be our effort and contribution to the final

conquest of Japan alongside our American Ally.

"For this Phase Two, there would be much long range air transport of troops and supplies from the UK to the Far East. In six years aircraft had grown in size and landing speeds and now needed landing strips of ever increasing length. Arthur Street, my fellow conspirator, prepared a powerful paper for the cabinet saying that by requisitioning under war powers the Fairey field and a large area beyond we could ensure a service airfield from which all our Phase Two needs could operate. I confess now that in our hearts we knew of several bomber airfields in the Home Counties which could have been made to do the job just as well. The paper came to the Cabinet who referred the issue to a committee under the Lord President, Sir John Anderson. The Committee met and I represented the Air Ministry. I found that Beaverbrook who was still in the Government was also a member. I took him into my confidence as to the real reason we were pressing for what we were sure was London's best chance of a great civil airport. He played up well.

"Rob. Hudson, Minister of Agriculture, put in a fierce objection on grounds that we were taking acres of the best market gardening ground. This I fear was very true. Ernest Brown, the Minister in charge of housing, joined Hudson in protest, saying we proposed to take land which had been earmarked for future housing schemes. I advanced as powerfully as I could the case for Phase Two needs. I did not dare to breathe the words 'Civil Aviation'. I put this right out of my mind so effectively that I really convinced myself of the priority of our case. The Cabinet came down on our side. We took the land. Hiroshima killed Phase Two. London Airport stands."

This account seems so improbable that it has been given little credence, being seen merely as the idle boasts of a vain old man on the edge of senility. [Balfour had strange ideas as to what would be considered praiseworthy. Another of his boasts was that as a fighter pilot in the 1914/18 war he had shot down a German observer balloon and deliberately killed the occupant when his unfortunate victim attempted to parachute to safety. His grounds for such callous behaviour were that the observer would have resumed his activities if he had been allowed to escape].

Balfour's account certainly does not correspond with the account given by Douglas Jay in his autobiography (16) in which he records, *"In my last months with the Ministry of Supply. I was asked to attend a meeting at the Air Ministry to decide on a site for a post-war civil airport, I protested at first that this was no business of mine at this stage of the war. But I was ordered to go and about six of us assembled at Assistant Secretary level. The meeting lasted forty minutes and we decided on Heathrow."* In the next sentence he contrasts the speed of that decision with the later search for a third airport site. *"In the 1960's and 1970's the Government and Parliament discussed for fifteen years the location of a third London Airport, spent several millions on public inquiries and by the late 1970's we had no new decision and no new airport".* Jay, ever a man to think that Whitehall knows best (he was later as President of the Board of Trade a leading proponent of Stansted), fails to realise that the agonising over the site of a third airport was due to the horrific environmental consequences of the decision to choose Heathrow as the site of the first airport.

The Air Ministry files make it abundantly clear that Balfour's account is substantially correct. It may well be that Jay was referring to a meeting which took place after the construction, ostensibly as a military airfield, was well under way.

The proposals for development envisaged construction in three stages, and at a meeting of the Anderson Committee (i.e. the one to which Balfour refers) a recommendation was passed on to the War Cabinet that approval to develop Stage 1 should be given. At a meeting two days later on 12 November 1943 the War Cabinet provisionally accepted this recommendation. This opened the way for the development to begin but, as will be seen later, there were still several difficulties to be overcome including worries about the legality of the action being taken. On this point advice was sought from the Treasury Solicitor in a minute dated 4 February 1944 which gives the information that, *"On the matter generally you should be aware that the ultimate object is to provide a suitable (civil) airport for London. Were there no other object it would be a question of Civil Aviation only and presumably Defence Regulations could not have been used for obtaining provision of land for use for normal peace-time purposes"*. The solicitor's reply is not preserved in the files but the minute leaves no doubt of the true intentions of those concerned within the Air Ministry who pursued their aim with a fanatical zeal even though it meant diverting valuable resources away from the war effort at a time when the preparation for the Normandy landings were well under way.

FACTORS INHIBITING THE DEVELOPMENT

Two factors inhibited the Air Ministry's proposals: one was the presence of the sludge disposal works at Perry Oaks, the other to a much lesser extent was the Fairey aerodrome. Three other factors which might be thought to have played a part, i.e. noise, agriculture and the fate of the inhabitants who were to be evicted from their homes, were completely ignored.

The Perry Oaks Problem

The proposals as approved at the first meeting involved the resiting of the Perry Oaks sludge disposal works. Figure 16, dated October 1943, shows the runways to be constructed as part of Stage 1 of the development in black. The main east-west runway on the map is further south of the Bath Road than at present with the sludge works being incorporated into the airport as part of the Stage 2 development.

The Defence of the Realm Act 1939 which was used to acquire the land for development allowed the authorities to requisition at short notice land deemed to be needed in connexion with the pursuit of the war without any right of appeal. In theory the sludge works could therefore have been acquired under the Act. But there was the practical difficulty that the works could not just be closed down; another site would have to be found. Long and ill-tempered negotiations were held with the Middlesex County Council which owned the works but the Council could see no possibility of finding an alternative site without resort to a public inquiry. This the Air Ministry was determined to avoid at all costs as an inquiry would have revealed the true reasons behind the acquisition of the land. Rather than face a public inquiry the Air Ministry revised the layout of the airport which avoided taking the works in the first instance. The frustration felt by the Ministry over the problem can be seen in the letter from the Ministry to the Middlesex County Council dated 1 May 1944 which says:

"I am directed to inform you that the increasing urgency of the need for an adequate airfield in the London area for the war requirements of the RAF and the inevitable delay which would arise in removal of your Council's sludge works from the Perry Oaks site has made it essential to adopt an amended lay-out which will avoid the immediate

necessity for interference with the land in your Council's possession .....

"It is anticipated that the extension of the airfield and consequently the removal of the sludge works will ultimately prove necessary and I am therefore to request that you will be good enough to continue your survey for a suitable site on which the sludge works could be provided and that you will advise the Department as soon as possible of any suitable site your enquiries may be able to find".

Forty five years later the survey for a suitable site still continues and it was only the presence of the sludge works that prevented (at least for the time being) the construction of a fifth terminal at Heathrow. In the intervening years responsibility for the works has passed from the Middlesex County Council to the Thames Water Authority. Cynics will not be surprised to learn that the present (1989) Chief Executive of the Thames Water Authority was formerly a member of the senior management of British Airways.

The problem of the Fairey Aerodrome.

The existence of the Fairey aerodrome also presented problems and it might be thought that, as members of the aviation community, the Fairey Aviation Company would have been given more sympathetic consideration than they in fact received. As the Company were manufacturers of military aircraft during wartime the Ministry of Aircraft Production would not agree to their eviction from their airfield without some alternative arrangement being made for their test flights. The arrangement reluctantly made for Fairey's was that on being expelled from their airfield at Heathrow they were to be given temporary permission to use Heston aerodrome which was reasonably close to their factory at Hayes. However, this arrangement did not last for long and in 1947 for the third time in their history they were evicted yet again by the Air Ministry. They ended up using White Waltham airfield in Berkshire, more than 20 miles away from Hayes. Sir Richard Fairey's gloomy prophecies described below proved to be well-founded and the Company was taken over by Westland Helicopters in 1960 which closed down Fairey's Hayes factory in 1972.

The effect of the prospective loss of their airfield on the Company can be judged from the correspondence that passed between Sir Richard Fairey, the founder of the Company, and his co-Chairman, Sir Clive Baillieu. Unfortunately for him, Fairey was out of the country at the time in his capacity as the Director-General of the British Air Mission in Washington. Fairey first learned officially of the news on 7 January 1944 and cabled, *"Decision so utterly calamitous, suggest liquidation only practical prospect. However, detailed reply coming quickest route"*. In his detailed reply Fairey wrote:

"Although as you say the matter may not have come as a complete surprise it was certainly a shock to me that such action could have been taken without prior consultation with us and that the powers-that-be should have taken a decision concerned with post-war activities that must inevitably affect the war effort. To suggest that the transfer of our flying centre during the war will not have its effect on our contribution to the war effort is little short of naivete .....

" I should have thought that after nearly thirty years in which the Company has not been altogether unhelpful to the Air Ministry and the Admiralty, whatever the ups and downs of its history, some regard for its future, if not gratitude for its past, might have induced some consideration for our interests.

"It is manifestly so much easier for the Civil Aviation authorities to look over the airports near London, that the foresight of private companies has made available, and then using government backing forcibly to acquire them, than to go to the infinite trouble that we had in making an aerial survey to find the site, buying the land from different owners, and then building up a fine airfield from what was market-gardening land.

"And why the haste to proceed? I cannot escape the thought that the hurry is not uninspired by the fact that a post-war government might not be armed with the power or even be willing to take action that is now being rushed through at the expense of the war effort".

Fairey then goes on in much detail about the various options facing the Company and concludes:

"You may think that I take a gloomy view. I have thought it out carefully and my mind keeps returning to that one question - how in the name of all that's reasonable can we transplant our Company, work-people and all, and simultaneously survive against our hungry competitors in finding new markets, unless the magician's wand can produce a new and suitable plant without disturbing our existing facilities in the process and into which we could move complete, within a space of a few weeks. My mind likewise concentrates on the fact that it is completely unnecessary for the Civil Aviation authorities to have their airport at Heathrow but it is vital to us. There are hundreds of airports in England, rapid transport by road and rail, to say nothing of helicopter, could easily be made available to them, and within reasonable limits, the further they are from London the better can they operate. The exact reverse applies to us".

Part of the problem facing the Company was that the Defence of the Realm Act allowed the Government to requisition land without paying compensation. The question of paying compensation dragged on for many years after the war as the Government took a very niggardly approach to the payment of proper compensation to the Company. The legal wranglings over compensation meant that Fairey's hangar at Heathrow could not be demolished until the question of compensation was settled. The hangar survived until the 1960's and was the last of the original buildings at Heathrow to be demolished.

The Noise Problem

In view of the major problems caused by aircraft noise it is quite extraordinary that there is no mention of noise anywhere in the files and the problem seems to have been entirely ignored. Colin Buchanan (17) has commented on this strange omission and one can do no better than to quote him on this:

"There were so many unbelievably noisy aircraft around in 1944 that it seems incredible that a so potent side-effect of aviation could have been overlooked. But overlooked it was. Heathrow was developed with a pair of parallel runways running due east-west pointing in one direction at point-blank range straight into the huge housing mass of West London and in the other direction, straight at Windsor only six miles away - Windsor of all places, historic town, royal residence, famous schools, glorious stretch of river, parks and gardens beyond compare. Heathrow is fifteen miles from the middle of London. This comparatively close proximity to the heart of a big city has presumably paid dividends over the years in respect of reduced travelling time to and from the airport, but the misery which the flight paths have spread, also over many years, far and wide over a huge part of London and the Home Counties, must surely make that decision in 1943 the most disastrous planning disaster to hit our country".

In addition to Windsor, Buchanan could well have added Hampton Court, Kew Gardens, Syon Park and Osterley Park to the list of historic and attractive places severely disturbed by overflying aircraft.

Aircraft noise consists of a build-up to a peak level, occurring at intervals, as opposed to the continuous but fluctuating noise from heavy traffic. The annoyance caused by aircraft depends on the peak perceived noise levels and on the number of aircraft heard within a given period. The index used in this country to define the annoyance is the so-called "noise and number index" (NNI) which is defined as:

$$NNI = \text{Average peak noise level} + 15\log_{10}N - 80$$

where N = number of aircraft heard in a defined period

Contours of noise exposure in terms of NNI can be mapped out around an airport in a similar manner to the contour lines used on maps to signify differences in height. An official committee set up to consider the problem of noise concluded that extensive annoyance is caused when the noise exposure exceeds 35 NNI and the noise becomes intolerable above the range 50-60 NNI. An exposure of 35 NNI corresponds to aircraft overflying at intervals of 15 minutes with intrusive levels of noise inside houses. 55 NNI means aircraft flying overhead at intervals of 1 - 2 minutes at noise levels which can interfere with conversation within houses.

It is estimated that 2.25 million people around Heathrow live within the 35 NNI contour which stretches from Maidenhead in the west to Fulham in the east. For those living close to the airport the situation is of course much worse and the Inspector reporting on the 4th Terminal Inquiry (described in Part 3) concluded that, *"In my view the present levels of noise around Heathrow are unacceptable in a civilised society"*.

Agricultural considerations

According to the Greater London Development Plan of 1944 (GLDP), *"Although the airport (Heathrow) is on land of first-rate agricultural quality, it is felt after careful consideration and thorough weighing-up of all the factors, that the sacrifice for the proposed purpose of the airport is justified"*. The GLDP was written after the decision to construct the airport had been made and was a government-sponsored publication. As Mandy Rice-Davies might have remarked, *"they would say that, wouldn't they"*.

In fact no consideration was given to the unique agricultural importance of the Heathrow area. This was the more reprehensible because as discussed in Part 1 Heathrow was at the very centre of the Thames Valley Market Gardening Plain. At a time of severe food shortages and stringent rationing this important market gardening area close to London should have been regarded as a valuable national resource and not one to be destroyed for the construction of an airport that could have been sited on land of lower agricultural potential.

The folly of destroying the valuable market garden land for the construction of an airport was well described by Dudley Stamp, the leading authority on land use and classification at the time. In a separate report (18) included in the GLDP he wrote:

"The brickearth is a magnificent soil - easily worked, adequately watered, of

high natural fertility and capable of taking and holding manure. It is a soil fit to be ranked with the world's very best.......In addition to the destruction of this good land by gravel digging a further using up has recently been made manifest where huge areas are taken for the construction of the airport. Was there ever such a profligate waste?"

The construction of Heathrow took the heart out of the West Middlesex market gardening industry which has been destroyed in less than a generation (9). It also changed the landscape from the pleasant agricultural scene described in Part 1 to one where the area could be described (19) in the following way:

"If there was an international prize for the ugliest urban landscape, some of the leading contenders would certainly be around a number of the world's leading airports. This is partly because airports have to be situated on flat land which does nothing to hide the acres of concrete and partly because, for safety reasons, tall trees that might soften the skyline are not tolerated. As the more affluent owners flee from the aircraft nuisance - a nuisance which affects eyes, ears and nose - neighbourhoods decline and take on an unloved appearance. What we finish up with all too frequently is an unappealing wasteland of warehouses, car parks and poor housing. Anyone who has had the misfortune to spend time around the airports of London, Paris and Chicago will recognise the picture all too well".

The fate of the inhabitants

The first official intimation of possible eviction of the local residents was the receipt of a letter from the Air Ministry in May 1943.

This was followed-up by a further letter giving notice to quit which was clearly intended to be sent in February 1944 but was not, in fact, posted until 2 May 1944. The delay in sending the second letter was undoubtedly due to the receipt on 12 February of Churchill's note to the Air Ministry, referred to in the next section, which led to a delay in final approval until 13 April.

The welfare of the people to be evicted to make way for the airport received scant consideration from the authorities. Many of them came from families who had lived in the Heathrow area for generations but they were treated worse than if they had been refugees from a foreign country. The Air Ministry was indeed loath to accept any responsibility for them at all and tried to get the Ministry of Health (then responsible for housing) and the local authorities to find alternative accommodation at a time when these bodies were desperately engaged on re-housing people whose houses had been destroyed by the V1 attacks on London. Faced with the refusal of these organisations to help, the Ministry even considered the possibility of forcibly billeting the unfortunate people in other houses in the area with all the problems that would have entailed. In the end the Ministry used accommodation already in its possession or in the possession of other service Ministries and most refugees from the Stage 1 development were re-housed at Heston in property adjoining the aerodrome. The feelings of the refugees as they left their homes for the last time are well summed-up by the lament written by one of them which is reproduced at the end of Part 1.

In the case of landowners their property was requisitioned, but not purchased, as the Defence Regulations envisaged that in many cases the requisitioned property would be returned to its original owners after the war. The owners were therefore paid a compensation rental by the Government on the supposition that they had let their land and property to the authorities for the

```
                    HOLBORN 3434
  TELEPHONE :
              Extn.                              AIR MINISTRY,
  Any communications on the
  subject of this letter should                  LONDON, W.C.2.
  be addressed to :—
     THE SECRETARY,
     and the following number                        May, 1943.
     quoted :—
              A.535303/43/W.6.b.(3).
```

Sir,
            I am directed to inform you that Air
Ministry have under consideration the construction
of an airfield in the Harmondsworth-Bedfont area, and
from a recent survey it appears that property in your
ownership or occupation is likely to be affected.
I have to state that this survey is only of a
preliminary nature and should it be decided to proceed
with the matter a further communication will be
addressed to you.

                    I am, Sir,
                        Your obedient Servant,

                        for Director of Lands & Requisitioning.

J.E.Wild, Esq.,
    Croft House,
      Cain's Lane,
        Heathrow Road,
          West Drayton,
            Middlesex.

Above: Letter dated May 1943 giving notice of Air Minstry's intentions
Right: Letter dated 2 May 1944 giving notice of eviction

TELEPHONE:
Temple Bar 5411
XXXHOLBORN 3434.
Extn. 9236

Any communications on the
subject of this letter should
be addressed to :—
THE UNDER SECRETARY
OF STATE, AIR MINISTRY,
and the following number
quoted :—
A.632131/44/W.6.b.3./R.88

Your Ref. ....

AIR MINISTRY,

LONDON, W.C.2.

2nd May
~~February~~, 1944.

Sir,

    Property at Heath Row.

  I am directed to inform you that the airfield at Heath Row is to be enlarged in the near future and it will be necessary for this purpose to take over your property possession of which, it is anticipated, will be required not later than 24-7-1944. Formal Notice of Requisition, in duplicate, is enclosed, one copy of which should be signed and returned in the accompanying franked envelope.

  Three copies of Claim Form 1, in respect of your interest as occupier, are also enclosed which, on completion, should be returned, in duplicate, to the Air Ministry. In this connection, it is pointed out that under Section 11 of the Compensation (Defence) Act, 1939, your claim must be lodged within six months from the date on which the compensation accrues due, that is, the date on which possession is taken, as otherwise it will not be entertained.

  Before any work is done on the property a Lands Officer will visit the site and discuss with you detailed arrangements for taking possession. Subject to essential Air Ministry requirements, every facility will be given to enable you to remove your movable property and effects and any growing crops.

  The property is being taken over under the Defence Regulations but this will not preclude sale and purchase by agreement if the Air Ministry decides that it is required for permanent retention.

  In conclusion, I am to draw attention to the fact that the Defence Regulations prohibit the making of any sketch, plan or other representation of any prohibited place. This prohibition applies to the making of any sketch or plan of R.A.F. Stations or defence works, etc., or the marking on any such sketch or plan of any Stations or works.

           I am, Sir,
           Your obedient Servant,

          B. Jarrett

     for Director of Lands and Requisitioning.

D.J. Wild, Esq.,
 Shrub End,
  Cains Lane,
   Heathrow Road,
    West Drayton.
     Middx.

duration of the war. In the case of Heathrow there was, of course, never any intention of returning the land to its rightful owners but the hypocritical pretence was made that it might be. Consequently the landowners did not receive proper compensation until well after the war and even then only at pre-war values.

Apart from this the terms of compensation were extremely harsh. One farmer, before he left, took away his greenhouses and sheds; the value of these was deducted from his eventual compensation even to the extent that the value of his front gate and hedge, which he also removed, was taken into account. Had he left them in place they would have been destroyed as they were of no value to the Air Ministry. The same attitude was adopted in awarding compensation for growing crops which were regularly inspected by the Air Ministry before the owners were evicted. In one case a deduction was made, *"because the crop (of broad beans) was seriously affected by black fly....... and my notes show that the crop of lettuce had not been watered".* As if a farmer would regularly spray his beans and water his lettuce when he knew full well that they were likely to be destroyed before they reached maturity!

When it came to finding accommodation for people being evicted for later developments, the Ministry and later the Ministry of Civil Aviation adopted the knock-on-the-door approach of personal interview to find the number of people involved and to ascertain their personal circumstances. The same callous attitude was adopted, as can be seen from a minute on the files addressed to the interviewers to the effect that, *"Initial contact made with occupiers is most important as the compensation finally paid is often affected by the antagonism or goodwill set up at the first meeting."*

The general feeling of helplessness in the face of the cold-hearted attitude first of the Air Ministry and later of the Ministry of Civil Aviation is well summed up in an editorial under the title "Wiped off the Map" in the Middlesex Advertiser and Gazette dated 5 December 1947:

"Wiped off the map"

"An atomic bomb dropped at Heathrow could not spread devastation more widely than the disruption caused by (the construction of an) airport on this spot. True the bomb would do it in no time at all, but the fact that the extension of the airport is to be effected in a matter of years only ensures that the sterilization will be more thorough. Ancient townships, valuable farmland, a huge section of the Great South West Road, every sort of building old and new, is to be swept utterly away and not even a living tree is to remain in seven square miles of the expanse thus blighted.

"Heathrow has gone, soon Sipson will be nothing but a memory and Harlington with its venerable buildings and fruitful orchards will be engulfed in turn. West Drayton, Harmondsworth, Stanwell and other communities are to suffer encroachment and their surviving portions will have the airport brought to their doorsteps with the shattering roar of transatlantic monsters.

"Where does the individual stand in all this - the farmer on his land, the family in the home, the worshipper in the church, all the units of life which have gone to the making of these English communities through the centuries?. It is frightening to find how little these considerations figure in the totalitarian thoroughness of the airport scheme. The very

hugeness of the project dwarfs the individual out of existence. If one public house were to be compulsorily closed there would be a public inquiry with KC's to fight for the licensee's rights; if a slum clearance were to be mooted the battle would rage for days with every individual interest involved. But with the airport the first consideration is, "The airport must be developed in stages and the construction of each stage should interfere as little as possible with its use." About the people on the land - nothing.

"The feeble protest which the local residents have been able to put up against the steam-roller of a Government Department has gained some grudging consideration. There may be pre-fabs or concrete houses for those driven from their homes which they need not accept if they don't want to. The Ministry of Civil Aviation itself will be the arbiter in the question of accommodation to be given in lieu.

"The same Ministry will also decide what compensation it is going to pay and it will take no responsibility for finding alternative sites for churches, shops, farms or businesses. From their decision in the interests of the airport there is no appeal, no impartial arbitration. It is as though a foreign country had conquered the land and were turning out its inhabitants.

"Is there no one to stand up to the Government in the interests of these people, peaceable Englishmen, whose only crime is that the land on which they live and work and which their fathers have defended through the centuries is coveted by a Government Department?."

This editorial refers specifically to the proposed evictions for the Stage 3 development north of the Bath Road which was eventually abandoned (see later) but it could well have been written at any time between 1944 and 1951.

Other problems

Although the problems of noise and the unfortunate inhabitants of Heathrow who faced eviction from their homes never even entered the minds of the Air Ministry, a problem that could not be ignored was a minute from the Prime Minister himself addressed to the Secretary of State for Air (Sir Archibald Sinclair) dated 12 February 1944. In this Churchill states,

"We ought not to withdraw 3000 men for this purpose (the development of the airport) until OVERLORD is over.....OVERLORD dominates the scene. I shall suggest to the Cabinet that the project be reconsidered in six months time..." (OVERLORD was the code name for the Normandy landings).

To the rather lame reply from Sinclair, Churchill retorted, *"I am not convinced. You always ask for everything. No one ever says 'No' to expenditure of men and money"*. Churchill's attitude caused consternation in the Air Ministry, which foresaw that if the project were to be delayed for six months from the Normandy landing the war in Europe could well be over and the reasons given for the development of Heathrow would disappear. Making a virtue of necessity the Air Ministry therefore put forward the revised plan which avoided the Perry Oaks sludge works, and Sinclair in a further minute to Churchill informed him that: *"A new scheme has been prepared, the essence of which is that by re-siting runways it enables us to meet war needs more quickly and with much less manpower during the OVERLORD period".*

Sinclair failed to reveal that the modified proposals meant, as the Air Ministry well knew, that if they eventually gained subsequent approval for the development of a civil airport one of the runways proposed in the revised plan would have to be demolished. This fact is clear from the reaction of the British Overseas Airways Corporation (BOAC) which was party to the plot and which complained about the unsuitability of the revised proposals for their civil aviation requirements. (The runway was built and subsequently abandoned without its ever having been used!)

In the early part of 1944 Churchill obviously had far more important things to worry about than the development of Heathrow and no doubt this was the reason why he eventually gave his reluctant consent. Following this, approval for the development was given at the meeting of the War Cabinet held on 13 April 1944. The Civil Aviation lobby in the Air Ministry had won and development started in June, the month of the Normandy landings and of the first V1 attacks on London. It shows the determination to push ahead at all costs with the project even if it meant diverting valuable resources away from the war effort.

THE STAGES OF DEVELOPMENT

The Air Ministry's proposals were to construct the airport in three stages. Stage 1 and 2 are shown in the map (Figure 16) which is dated October 1943. This map shows the runways to be constructed as part of Stage 1 of the development in black. The extensions of the runways which would have occurred in Stage 2 are shaded. The proposals involved the removal of the Perry Oaks sludge disposal works. The difficulty of finding an alternative site for the sludge works without holding a public inquiry led to these proposals being abandoned.

Stage 3 was put forward at the first meeting held, on 10 August 1943, of the Departmental Committee which had been set up to consider the development of Heathrow. At that meeting a completely new plan for the development was proposed. It involved moving the site to the north and centering it on the Bath Road. However it was considered that although this scheme had considerable merits, *"no Government would be prepared to consider a project that involved razing the three old world villages of Harmondsworth, Sipson and Harlington to the ground"*, and the matter of a possible Stage 3 development was not pursued at that time. (As will be seen later this rebuff did not put an end to the proposal which was later raised again and eventually gained approval).

Work on the construction of Stage 1, as modified to avoid the sludge disposal works at Perry Oaks, began in June 1944. The proposals as approved for Stages 1 and 2 involved the demolition of 117 houses, 8 factories or places of work other than farms, and the eviction of 500 people. The schedule of dispossessions for Stage 1 was:

Date	Farm Houses	Dwelling Houses	Cottages
1.6.44	-	-	2
15.6.44	3	2	1
1.8.44	2	2	6
15.9.44	4	5	16
1.11.44	3	11	3
2.2.45	4	3	7
Total	15	23	35

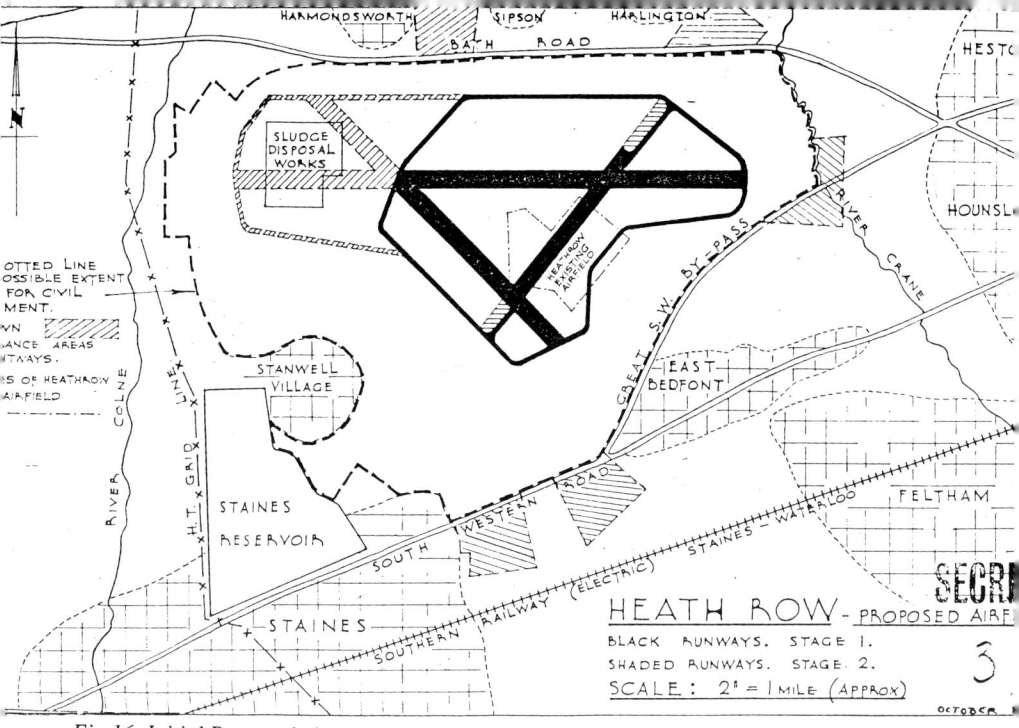

Fig 16. Initial Proposals for the Airport 1943

The dispossessions involved the demolition of all buildings south of the Bath Road from Harlington Corner to Longford with the exception of those close to, or facing on to, the Bath Road and those in the Perry Oaks area.

The firm of George Wimpey Ltd. was appointed as the main contractor and at a time of acute labour shortage the labour force had to be largely recruited from Ireland. This fact is probably the origin of the witticism that WIMPEY is simply an acronym of "We Import More Paddies Each Year".

Stage 1 had not been completed when the airport was transferred from the Air Ministry to the Ministry of Civil Aviation (MCA) on 1 January 1946. Despite all the spurious claims about the urgent RAF need, the airport had never been used by the RAF and the first use of the airport was for a civil flight, which took place for publicity purposes, when a British South American Airways Lancastrian took off on a long distance proving flight to South America. The airport was formally opened on 31 May 1946.

Before the transfer of the airport to the MCA a Cabinet Committee on Civil Aviation had been set up. This Committee recommended that the name of the airport should be changed from "Heathrow" to "London Airport" on the grounds that "Heathrow" was difficult for most foreigners to pronounce (the Committee rejected the fatuous recommendation made earlier that the airport should be renamed "St.George's Airport"). The Committee also revised the proposed stages of development; three stages were still envisaged but these differed considerably from the previous proposals. The stages now planned were:

Stage 1. This was to be completed by 31.12.47 and involved the compulsory purchase of all the land required for the airport south of the Bath Road.

Page 47

THE HISTORY OF HEATHROW

This meant the acquisition of 2650 acres of land including the 1590 acres requisitioned by the RAF under the Defence of the Realm Act, and the demolition of 215 houses.

Stage 2. This was to be completed by 31.12.49 and did not involve any further acquisition of land or buildings.

Stage 3. This was to be completed in the period 1950/53 and involved the resurrection of the proposals to extend the airport north of the Bath Road. It included the purchase of 1600 acres of land and the re-housing of the occupants of 950 houses (for presentational reasons the Committee decided to refer to the number of houses rather than the number of people, which was in excess of 3000).

The proposals for Stage 3 were agreed by the Cabinet on 10 January 1946 and are shown in Figure 17. They involved the complete destruction of Sipson and the greater part of Harlington. The map shows that the proposed northern boundary approximately follows the line of the M4 motorway which was conceived in 1946 as a replacement for the Bath Road which would have had to be closed.

The original proposals included the demolition of the ancient parish church of Harlington which dates back to the XIIth century and has the finest

Fig 17. Proposals for the extended Airport 1946

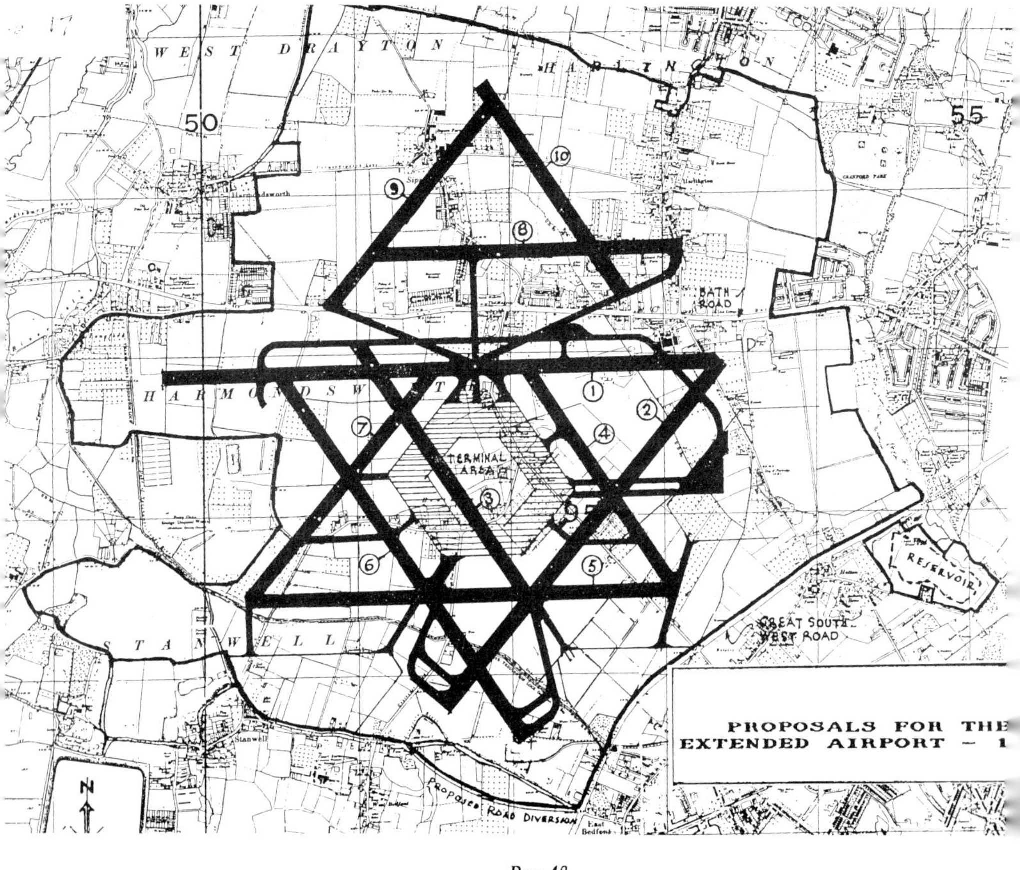

Norman doorway in Middlesex. This raised strong objections from the Diocese of London and the Royal Commission on Historical Monuments. To overcome these objections the absurd suggestion was made that the church should be dismantled stone-by-stone and rebuilt on another site - Twickenham was suggested but it is not clear why. Eventually it was agreed that there was no need to demolish the church and Figure 17 shows an enclave on the north-east boundary of the extended airport where the boundary was re-adjusted round the church.

When Stage 3 was announced in 1946 no firm dates were given as to when the extension of the airport to the north of the Bath Road would take place. By 1948 serious delays were occurring with the development of the airport and concern was being expressed about the costs. The date of the extensions was therefore deferred to 1955 at the earliest. A sarcastic editorial in the Middlesex Advertiser and Gazette of 27 August 1948 referred to these delays thus:

"What an agreeable and satisfying experience is the planning on paper of a big project. You take a map of an area seven square miles in extent, and having decided to your own satisfaction what are the difficulties to be overcome, you proceed to draw on it runways, taxiways, aprons and so on where the map shows farms, villages and roadways. Then you say, 'presto this shall be an airport' and sit back and expect it to happen. If someone ventures to ask, what about the cost, whence are the the labour and materials to come, where are the displaced persons to go, what of the valuable land and resources diverted from essential production, you blandly reply that such considerations are not in your terms of reference.

Looking again at the report of the Layout Panel of London Airport one gets the idea that it was conceived in such a fashion. There was an easy optimism about it which assumed that the first stage of the plan was already completed, that the second stage was to be finished in 1949 and the third was to be completed by 1953. That was twenty months ago, and already it is being discovered how little account had been taken of realities. In fact the first stage is still in progress having got little beyond the three runways at Heathrow constructed by the RAF; the second stage, only just begun has run into difficulties because of the capital cuts imposed to regulate the scarce manpower and labour; the third stage cannot get going before 1953 if at all.

A touch of realism is brought to the project by the recent report of the Select Committee called into being when it was seen things were not going according to plan. Yet even in this report there is a frightening disregard of the public, who have nothing to do with the Airport except to bear its cost and suffer its inconveniences. The huge runways are spread out over the countryside, flattening villages, eating up farmland and destroying roadways, and for all this loss to themselves the public, by the mad reckoning which passes for political economy in these days, have to foot the bill, so that they have to pay at both ends.

The Select Committee heard no witnesses from the doomed villages of Sipson and Harlington, made no inquiry into the loss of production on the requisitioned lands and no one has attempted to estimate the extra cost imposed on road transport by the proposed diversion of the Bath Road. The Airport as at present planned is a monstrous prodigality...."

Throughout the period 1948 - 1950 the uncertainty as to when or whether the airport would be extended continued. In October 1950 the Ministry of Civil Aviation announced that it had revised its plans for the airport extension. The revised plan (Figure 18) invoved a smaller area of land and reprieved parts of Harlington and Sipson. However, Harmondsworth which hitherto had been just outside the threatened area now found itself a potential victim.

Figure 18 shows the proposals which included an extraordinary "wedge" of land in which houses in Harmondsworth were to remain although cut

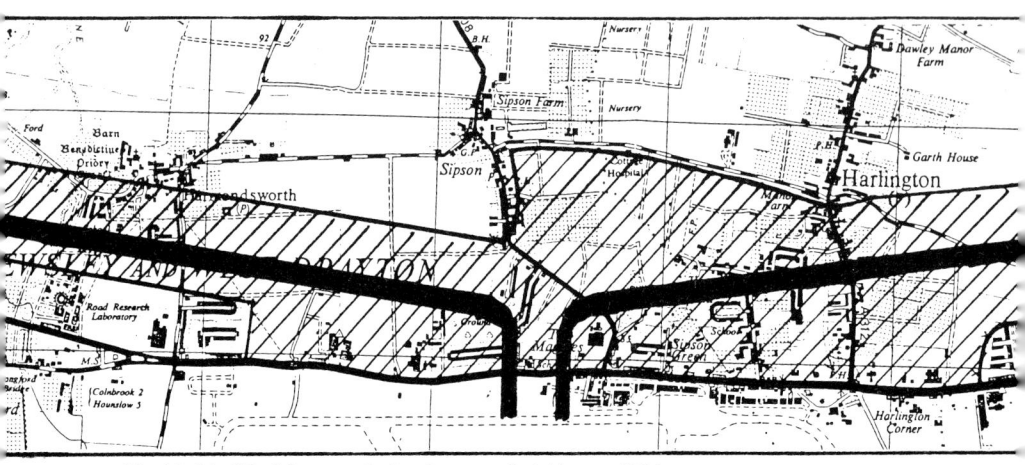

Fig 18. Modified Proposals for the extended Airport 1950

off from the rest of the village and surrounded by the airport on three sides. The map is also remarkable for the manner in which the proposed boundary of the airport was drawn to exclude residential areas. This was, no doubt, for the best of reasons but the environment of the residents had the extensions been built does not bear thinking about. It shows yet again the total failure of the authorities to have any regard for the amenities of the residents of the Heathrow area which has characterised their attitude from the beginning.

The residents of Harmondsworth now found themselves allied with those of Sipson and Harlington in resisting the development. The resistance compared with the later anti-airport campaigns at Cublington and Stansted was strangely muted. There was undoubted resentment but a curious apathy prevailed, no doubt inherited from the war-time years when people had become conditioned to being directed and told what to do by the authorities. The general feeling seemed to be that if the Ministry had made up its mind nothing could stop it. At a public meeting one view expressed was that, *"it would be un-British to resist a development that the Government had declared was in the public interest"* although at the same meeting the Vicar of Harmondsworth declared that, *"although he did not mind having a church without a steeple he would fight any development which meant that he had a church without people"*.

Although the effect of the proposals on the threatened area was calamitous the Ministry refused to consider any compensation for owners or occupiers of property in advance of the property being requisitioned. Moreover it declared that compensation would be at pre-war values and would not take account of price rises due to the scarcity of housing in post-war years. As a result only the most urgent repairs were carried out to the houses affected (950 at first, 665 after the proposed stage 3 had been modified). The situation was particularly serious for owner-occupiers who found themselves in a position of being unable to sell when they wanted to move house.

Throughout 1951 and the early part of 1952 the Ministry of Civil Aviation continued with its cat-and-mouse policy of threatening to come north of the Bath Road but refusing to say when, other than that it would not be before 1955. By mid 1952, however, doubts were beginning to be expressed as to whether the airport would ever be extended across to the north side of the Bath Road and in December 1952 the Ministry finally announced that the scheme had been abandoned.

The futility of the years of uncertainty was well summed-up in the editorial of the Middlesex Advertiser and Gazette of 19 December 1952 :

"*For over six years there has been an intermittent controversy regarding the effect of London Airport plans on the communities settled in the land to be occupied. Every now and then there would be a "final" revision of the plan to add impetus to the controversy. The Government's decision last week (to abandon the plan) makes it plain that the grandiose scheme for the airport as first planned was adopted too easily without due regard to the consequences to the people it was proposed to disturb. Now that the part of the plan for the northern side of the Bath Road has been found to be not needed, all the anxiety and loss which has been the lot of the inhabitants of the threatened area over the past six years is shown to have been unnecessary and it could have been avoided if there had been more consideration and earlier consultation with the people concerned.*"

The same editorial also has some harsh things to say about public apathy and the lack of support for the resistance groups formed to fight the extension of the airport. Some of these groups, now transformed into residents' and amenity associations, survive and like to think that they were responsible for preventing the development. In fact as the editorial goes on to say:

"*The case for the inhabitants (and those concerned are in an area far larger than the actual site proposed for the airport) has had far too feeble support from the public. There have been a few valiant fighters but they have lacked the strong public backing sufficient to impress the authorities. The few have stuck to their guns but it would be a mistake to assume that the Government has capitulated to their protestations. The reason for the Government's decision is that the extension of the Airport is no longer considered necessary, and that is something entirely different*".

With the reprieve from the death sentence the villages around the airport were sentenced to life imprisonment with the airport as their neighbour. How this has affected the area around Heathrow is considered in Part 3.

Middlesex Advertiser and Uxbridge Gazette

BUCKINGHAMSHIRE ADVERTISER
"ESTABLISHED IN 1840 AS BRIDGEWATER'S JOURNAL"
The Old-Established

Vol. CX. No. 5856

FRIDAY, DECEMBER 19, 195[?]

Bentalls Values are on page 7

'THE MOST WONDERFUL CHRISTMAS BOX WE'VE EVER HAD'

In the slipstream of the Airport news: thousands rejoice and give thanks

REJOICING and thanksgiving, following the news in last week's Advertiser-Gazette that London Airport will not be extended north of the Bath-road, has been in evidence this week all over the affected area.

A psychological "dead hand" has been lifted. Dozens of people interviewed all made the same general comment — "it's the most wonderful Christmas present we've ever had."

For years many thousands of people, firms, and or[...]

MORE LIGHT BUT—

He is not very partial to gas

COUNCILLOR ROUGH does not like gas — not the kind in evidence at council meetings, but the kind used for street lighting.

PART 3

DEVELOPMENTS 1952 - 1988

ANCILLARY DEVELOPMENTS

For some years after the decision was made to abandon the proposed development of the airport to the north of the Bath Road all official attention was concentrated on completing the airport to the original plans. This was not surprising, as the development had fallen well behind schedule and the escalating costs were a persistent source of concern. In 1953 the decision was taken to develop Gatwick as a second airport for London to take flight diversions from Heathrow during bad weather and at peak flying times.

These developments were obviously enough to be going on with as far as official action was concerned. However, as David McKie has pointed out (20) there are two other effects of the creation of a modern airport that are of equal significance to the noise problem. They both result from the ripple effects of siting a landing strip in the middle of a stretch of countryside. The first is the physical effect, not only on the area of the airport itself, but on a huge swath all around it. The second is the economic effect - the creation not just of thousands of new jobs for people dependent on the airport but of a host of other new commercial openings created by those industries which home in on an airport like a moth on a flame.

The first of these ancillary effects to become apparent was the demand for off-airport parking, followed by a proliferation of hotels on the airport perimeter. The Skyways Hotel on the Bath Road, which opened in 1959, was the first hotel to appear. This was built on the site of Bedford Lodge, a Georgian house which stood in a large garden. It was but the first example of the replacement of an old existing building in sympathy with its surroundings by modern systems-built blocks of no architectural merit (compare Figures 19 and 20). It was followed, in 1961, by the Ariel Hotel built on the site of the "Coach and Horses", an 18th century inn needlessly demolished to make way for it (Figure 21). Since then many other hotels too numerous to mention have been built mostly on the Bath Road frontage of the airport. The major exception to this was the construction of the Post House hotel in the heart of the Green Belt between Harlington and Harmondsworth which, to the dismay of the local planning authority, was allowed on appeal in 1969. The report of the Inspector (21) recommending that the appeal should be allowed stated that, "*An hotel, standing about 120 feet, would do no violence to any part of the M4 or its surroundings*". Readers can judge for themselves the truth of this astonishing claim from Figure 22. In the autumn of 1962 work started on the construction of the M4 motorway with a spur road linking the M4 to the centre of the airport. As described in Part 2 the motorway had originally been conceived as a replacement for the Bath Road and was originally to have been the northern

Above: Fig 19 Ash Cottage, Harlington Corner 1967
Below: Fig 20. Ibis Hotel, Harlington Corner 1988 *(Built on the site of Ash Cottage)*

boundary of the airport. The road opened to traffic in 1965 and has been another significant factor in attracting commercial developments to the Heathrow area.

THE FOURTH TERMINAL

Up to 1970 the only expansion of the airport outside the perimeter set in 1952 was the extension of the northern runway to the west, approval for the construction of which was given in 1967. During the 1960's and early 70's it was becoming apparent that Heathrow and Gatwick as they had been planned would no longer be able to cope with the anticipated expansion of air traffic. This set in motion the long-running saga of the search for a site for the third London airport which is well described in References 17, 20 and 22.

The cancellation in 1974 of the proposal to construct the third London Airport at Foulness (Maplin) increased pressure on Heathrow. Proposals were therefore made, in the mid-1970's, to expand the capacity of Heathrow by constructing a fourth terminal on the southern side of the airport outside its existing perimeter. The first mention of a possible fourth terminal was in the Maplin review paper published in July 1974, and the Heathrow Master Development Plan published in March 1976 by the British Airports Authority (BAA) included the construction of the fourth terminal as a specific commitment.

A planning application for the construction of the terminal was submitted by the BAA to the local planning authority in September 1977. Because of its far-reaching implications this application was "called-in" by the Department of the Environment which decided that a public inquiry should be held. The inquiry, the first ever to have been held over any development at Heathrow, opened on 31 May 1978 and closed on its 93rd day on 15 December. The result was, of course, a foregone conclusion. In his report (23) the Inspector stated that, "*In my*

Fig 21. "Coach and Horses" and Ariel Hotel 1961

Fig 22. Post House Hotel 1988. ("An hotel standing about 120 feet, would do no violence to the M4 or its surroundings" - Appeal decision 1969 (reference 21)).

view the present levels of noise around Heathrow are unacceptable in a civilised society", but this did not stop him from recommending that permission for the construction of a fo n of the airport should be given, the Inspector did go on to say:

"In the past the growth of Heathrow untrammelled by normal planning control has appeared to proceed without proper consideration for its effect on the environment, especially in relation to noise. There is an inevitable danger that permission for T4 should be seen by some as yet another instance of precedence being given to the interests of travellers by air over the enjoyment of life by the local population. If this impression is to be dispelled it is, in my view, essential that if they decide to permit T4 the Secretaries of State should re-iterate that it is the Government's policy that there will be neither a fifth terminal nor any other major expansion of Heathrow."

The Government accepted these recommendations and it became official policy that once the fourth terminal was completed no further expansion would be permitted. With such an unequivocal undertaking from the Government it might reasonably be thought that the matter had been finally decided and, if further airport capacity was needed in the future, it would certainly not be at Heathrow. Within less than four years events were to prove otherwise.

THE FIFTH TERMINAL

The Government's pledge not to expand Heathrow beyond a fourth terminal (which open ..' to traffic in 1986), coupled with the growth in air traffic, increased the demand for a third London airport which had been shelved by the Maplin review. In the time-scale available it was decided that expansion of Stansted would be the optimum solution because it already had a suitable runway. This was despite the fact that the Roskill Commission had extensively investigated a site for the third airport and had decisively rejected Stansted as unsuitable (20).

Not surprisingly the Stansted resistance groups which had been fighting the expansion of Stansted for the past 25 years re-mustered their forces to fight yet again.

In December 1979 the BAA was invited by the Government to submit proposals for the development of Stansted and this plan was submitted in July 1980. Lobbying against these proposals then began in earnest; the main opponents were (needless to say) the anti-Stansted lobby which had the ungainly acronym NWEEHPA (North West Essex and East Hertfordshire Preservation Association) and British Airways which did not fancy the prospect of having to fly from three airports. British Airways proposed instead that the demand could be met by the construction of a fifth terminal at Heathrow. This was seized on by NWEEHPA which persuaded Uttlesford District Council, the local planning authority for the Stansted area, to submit a planning application for the construction of a fifth terminal at Heathrow on the site of the Perry Oaks sludge works.

The so-called NIMBY (Not In My Back Yard) syndrome is a well-known factor at public inquiries where people naturally wish to protect their own environment. This is understandable, and although a protest group is saying in effect that the development should go elsewhere, most would hesitate before they identified a specific alternative site where other people would have to put up with the consequences. This is just what NWEEHPA did by campaigning for further development at Heathrow instead of at Stansted and is almost without precedent among environmental protest movements.

The application by Uttlesford District Council was supported by British Airways but opposed by the BAA which kept (at least at first) to the Government's policy of restricting the further expansion of Heathrow. The submission of the application meant that the terms of reference of the inquiry into the expansion of Stansted had to be extended to include the possible construction of a fifth terminal at Heathrow. This set the scene for the airports inquiries (24); these inquiries started at Stansted on 21 September 1981 and ended there after 175 working days on 26 October 1982. They then resumed at Heathrow on 11 January 1983 for a further 83 working days until 5 July 1983.

The Inspector's report (24) in a massive nine volumes was published in 1984. The report recommended that Stansted should be expanded and this recommendation was later accepted by the Government. The anti-Stansted campaigners had thus lost the final battle in a war they had been fighting for 25 years during which they had won most of the previous battles. In recommending the expansion of Stansted the Inspector also recommended that:

" The two applications made by Uttlesford District Council for planning permission for the Extension of Heathrow Airport to provide a new passenger terminal complex and associated facilities and works on land at Heathrow Airport and Perry Oaks Sludge Disposal Works be refused."

However, the Inspector further recommended that:

"Immediate Government and other action be taken to ensure that the Perry Oaks sludge treatment works is removed and that the site of the works, together with other necessary land to the west of the boundary with the M25, be taken into Heathrow Airport with the object of providing a fifth passenger terminal complex and other airport development with direct access to the motorway as soon as possible".

Thus in their defeat the anti-Stansted lobby had ensured, without gaining any benefit for themselves, that the possibility of further expansion of Heathrow was kept on the agenda; this despite the strong recommendation, endorsed by the Government, at the T4 inquiry that no such expansion should take place. Graham Eyre, the Inspector at the T5 inquiry, had none of his predecessor's qualms and, in his report, he criticised the T4 inquiry Inspector for making such a recommendation. He went to great lengths to make it clear that the only reason he had recommended that permission for the construction of a fifth terminal should be refused was because:

"*It is unlikely that additional passenger terminal capacity could be constructed, commissioned and in operation at Heathrow in less than a decade from the date of decision to relocate Perry Oaks......Perry Oaks must be moved as expeditiously as possible, it must unquestionably go and its existence cannot reasonably be advanced as a reason for rejecting the expansion of Heathrow beyond four terminals*".

Since the Inspector's report was published work has started on the expansion of Stansted. But the sludge works at Perry Oaks still (1988) receives its regular quota of sludge from Mogden sewage works, as it has ever since 1935, even though the Air Ministry had told its then owners in 1944 that, "*the extension of the airfield and consequently the removal of the sludge works will ultimately prove necessary*". From time to time reports appear of negotiations between BAA and the Thames Water Authority about the removal of the sludge works but there seems little possibility of a fifth terminal being completed on the Perry Oaks site in this century. Construction cannot even begin before the sludge works has been closed down, and this cannot be done until a solution is found for the disposal of the sludge from Mogden which clearly has to go somewhere.

The existing method is a very cheap and efficient method of treating waste. At Perry Oaks the sludge is allowed to decompose naturally, which leads to a large reduction in its volume and weight and changes the sludge into a product which is easy to handle and no longer offensive. The alternatives to a land-based sludge works are dumping at sea or incineration and both give rise to problems. Sludge dumping around the coasts of Britain is under strong criticism within the EEC because of fears about pollution, and was cited as a possible cause of the deaths of seals in catastrophic numbers in 1988. Incineration is extremely expensive and can give rise to air pollution. If another land-based site is selected, it must be reasonably close to Perry Oaks or Mogden, and any proposals for an alternative would meet strong local resistance, as a sludge works is almost as unwelcome a neighbour as is an airport.

THE PRESSURES FOR FURTHER DEVELOPMENT
Airport expansion

Even before the expansion of Stansted has been completed there have been vociferous demands for still further increase in airport capacity in the south-east. A recent (January 1989) forecast of the growth of air traffic made by the Department of Transport predicted that the number of passengers at all British airports could treble by the year 2005. In the case of Heathrow, passenger capacity was estimated to jump by about 20 million to 55 million passengers a year implying the need for a fifth terminal and the possibility of a third main runway. These figures are never questioned yet, without a touch of insanity, how is it possible to imagine trebling the number of passengers? let alone the appalling environmental consequences of trying to meet such a ludicrous level of demand.

Perhaps the most extreme demand for further expansion of Heathrow has come from the Air Transport Users' Committee (ATUC), the Chairman of which at his Annual Press Conference in 1987 (25) declared:

"*We do not want to ride roughshod over the interests of those living around airports. Equally we do not accept that they should ride roughshod over the interests of millions who want or need to travel whether on holiday or business......To meet the burgeoning demand for both passengers and cargo users it is surely possible to construct an additional commuter runway at Heathrow between the M4 and A4 or a second runway at Gatwick to the south of the present one.*"

When the Chairman of the ATUC speaks of the interests of those who want to travel on holiday he fails to recognise that social and personal tranquillity require various restraints on the free market. There is a burgeoning demand for drugs, but the Government quite properly rides roughshod over the interests of drug addicts and restricts the availability of drugs because of the harmful consequences of free access. The further expansion of Heathrow would undoubtedly increase demand for air travel, but, if through a shortage imposed by considerations of nuisance air travel from Heathrow became more expensive, travellers would soon find alternative forms of transport or fly from less fashionable airports.

Although the ATUC statement refers to a second runway at Gatwick, this possibility has been ruled out by a legally binding agreement in 1979 between the BAA and West Sussex County Council precluding the construction of a new runway for at least 40 years. Stansted is being developed to handle 8 million passengers a year but there is pressure to raise this to the intended 25 million by the end of the century. If this does not suffice, and there are indications that it will not, there may indeed be pressure to build a third east-west runway at Heathrow.

If there were to be a third E-W runway, to the north it would have to be about a mile from the existing northern runway to allow for independent operation but not so close to the M4 as to be a danger to traffic on the motorway. To the east it could not cross the spur road linking the airport centre with the M4. To the west the numerous distributaries of the River Colne as it crosses Harmondsworth Moor and the proximity of the M4/M25 interchange would make construction difficult. This leaves the only possible site for a third runway as that shown in Fig 23.

Linking the runway shown in this figure with the remainder of the airport would inevitably mean the total destruction of the villages of Sipson and Harmondsworth and bring about a massive increase in the number of people severely disturbed by aircraft noise. Presumably the Chairman of the ATUC would not regard this as riding roughshod over the interests of those living near the airport.

On the face of it this seems to be such a preposterous proposal that it cannot be taken seriously. Yet the whole manner in which Heathrow has been allowed to develop is preposterous, but this has not stopped its continued expansion. So far the proposal has only been made by the ATUC, but when asked to confirm or deny plans for the expansion of Heathrow to the north of the A4 the BAA has merely stated that consideration of a third runway at Heathrow is premature.

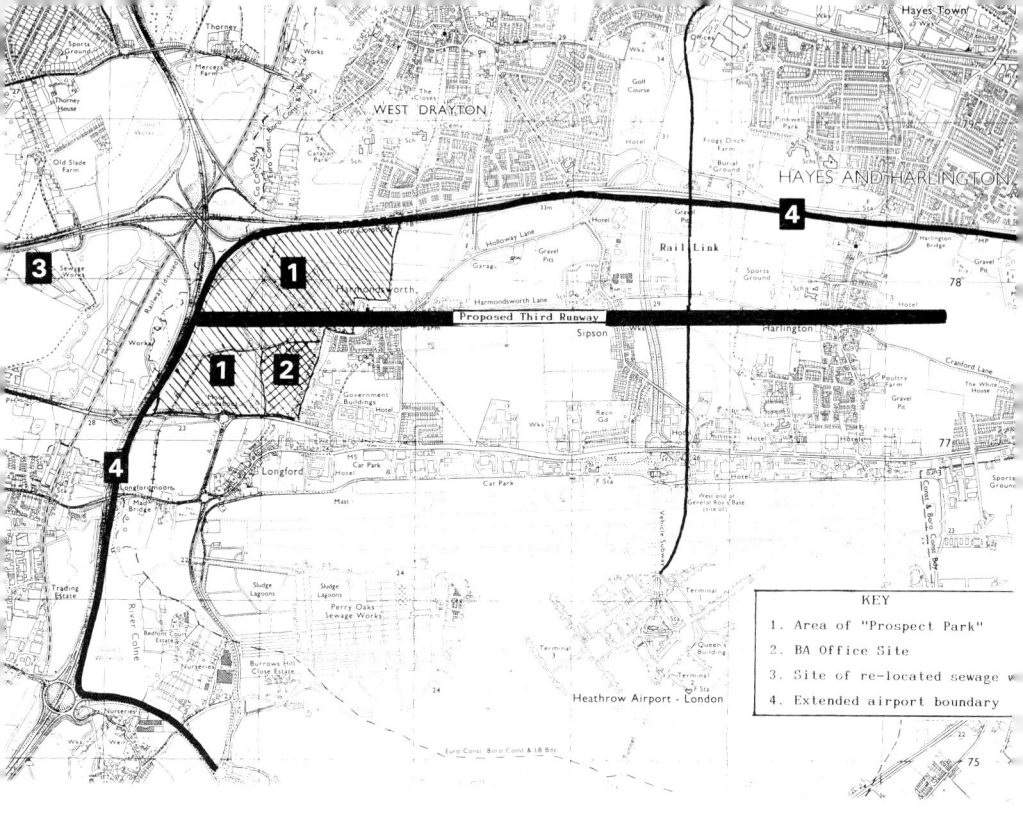

Fig 23. Possible location for a new runway at Heathrow and a new rail link with Paddington. (Based on Ordanace Survey with the permission of the Controller of HMSO. Crown copyright reserved).

Surface access

From the opening of the M4 with a spur road to Heathrow in 1964 until the completion of the M25 in 1985 little was done to improve road access to the airport. Within a short time of opening the M25 was loaded to capacity during peak periods so that between Heathrow and Gatwick work had to be started almost at once to provide a fourth lane. Even this seems unlikely to satisfy demand and serious proposals, have been made without a hint of sarcasm, to construct another road on top of the M25.

To help relieve road congestion to the airport an extension to the Piccadilly line from Hounslow West to the airport was opened in 1976. This had little adverse environmental effect as the line runs underground for almost its entire length. This line provides direct access to central London with a travelling time of 45 minutes, but unfortunately the trains are not suited to the carriage of passengers with a large amount of luggage nor can they be adapted. Proposals were therefore made in 1988 to connect the airport to the British Rail mainline into

Paddington which could provide a high-speed non-stop service.

The route, as originally proposed by its sponsors (British Rail and BAA), would have run along existing lines from Paddington to Hayes before turning south to the airport, crossing the M4 and running between Sipson and Harlington (Figure 23). The line was to have been above ground, crossing the M4 on a 6-metre high viaduct, and gradually coming down to ground level before going underground between Sipson Lane and the Bath Road.

An examination of Figure 23 suggests that the designers were not capable of anything more complicated than a straight line. An above-ground route was chosen because it was cheaper than the underground alternative even though the environmental advantages of choosing the latter are self-evident. Nobody who has read this account thus far will be surprised to learn that approval for the proposal was sought by way of a Parliamentary Private Bill rather than being considered at a Public Inquiry. The proposals were opposed by Hillingdon Council which commissioned a firm of consultants to prepare an alternative route which would have less damaging environmental effects.

The consultants suggested an alternative route which would leave the main line at Southall and go underground all the way to Heathrow. This alternative, which would do little environmental damage, was rejected by British Rail and BAA on the grounds that it was too costly, although the additional sum of £10 million on top of the £190 million already committed seems a small price to pay for organisations as large as the sponsors. They therefore persisted in taking their original plan through Parliament. The proposals were, however, rejected by the House of Lords in May 1989, mainly on account of the damage it would have done to agricultural land in the Green Belt between Sipson and Harlington. The latest proposal from British Rail is that more (about 4 miles) of the route shown in Figure 23 should be underground, with a tunnel under the M4, so as not to fragment the Green Belt. The House of Lords Select Committee, which rejected the original plans, has indicated that the proposed amendment rectifies the essential objections which it expressed previously. However, people living in the streets off Bourne Avenue, Hayes, would still have high speed trains thundering past their homes from early morning to late evening. Consequently Hillingdon Council is still opposed to the scheme and has announced that it will continue to advocate the alternative underground route from Southall.

EPILOGUE

Much of the report of the T5 inquiry (24) reads like a eulogy for civil aviation and the Inspector recommended far more development than even aviation interests had asked for. However, few could disagree with his following statement:

"The history and development of airports policy on the part of administration after administration of whatever political colour has been characterised by ad hoc expediency, unacceptable and ill-judged procedures, ineptness, vacillation, uncertainty and ill-advised and precipitate judgements. Hopes of a wide sector of the regional population have been frequently raised and dashed. A strong public cynicism has inexorably grown. Political decisions in this field are no longer trusted. The consequences are grave. There will now never be a consensus. Other important policies which do not countenance substantial expansion of airport capacity or new airports have been allowed to develop and have become

deeply entrenched. Somewhat paradoxically, such policies are heavily relied upon by thousands of reasonable people who strongly object to airport development. The past performance of Governments guarantees that any decision taken now will provoke criticism and resentment on a wide scale. I do not level this indictment merely as gratuitous criticism nor in order to fan the fires of the long history of controversy, but to set the context for current decisions which will shape a future that must enjoy an appropriate measure of certainty and immutability".

POSTSCRIPT

Introduction

This book was written in 1987/88 with a few late additions when the book was about to go to the printers. Since then there have been a large number of developments that mean that much of the narrative in Part 3 has been overtaken by events. By early 1993 the original stocks of the book had been exhausted but it was still in demand. Two possible solutions to meeting the continued demand for the book were considered. One was to reprint the original text unchanged. The other was to prepare a completely new edition to take account of additional information gained since Parts 1 and 2 were written and of developments that had occurred since Part 3 was written.

With so many proposals for the further development at Heathrow under review, preparation of a second edition would only temporarily solve the problem of keeping the book up-to-date. At the same time merely reprinting the original text would mean that the original Part 3 would become increasingly irrelevant. It was therefore decided that, as a compromise, this Postscript should be added to the original draft. This takes account of developments in the period 1989-1993 and of the proposals for possible further development. It does this by expanding the descriptions, already given in Part 3, of the three subjects of the fifth terminal, airport expansion and surface access.

It is to be hoped that it will eventually be realised that we cannot simply go on extrapolating ever-rising forecasts of growth in air traffic indefinitely into the future without unacceptable environmental consequences. As a Society we will need to pay a higher price for air travel to offset the unacceptable disturbance that is caused by the civil aviation industry. Until such time is reached it will never prove possible to write a history of Heathrow that will remain up-to-date for very long.

P.T.Sherwood
March 1993

"Prospect Park"

The recent acquisition by British Airways of some 275 acres of land on Harmondsworth Moor of what it is pleased to call "Prospect Park" just outside the airport perimeter, potentially represents the first major incursion of the airport into the area north of the Bath Road (A4). This land has been ostensibly acquired so that BA can build Headquarters Offices (or what it refers to as its Corporate Business Centre) for itself on 15 acres in one corner and in return the Company has agreed to lay-out the remaining land as public parkland - hence the name "Prospect Park". A name which incidentally has no geographic or historical significance and is merely a figment of BA's imagination. The areas in question are shown in Figure 23.

Up to the recent decision on Prospect Park the airport had been largely kept within its pre-1952 boundaries. There have been exceptions, which are discussed in pages 53-56, and many of these have had adverse environmental effects. However, in terms of area, as compared with the vast area of the airport, they cannot be regarded as significant. The proposals to construct a fifth terminal and a third runway, which are considered later, would, of course, greatly expand the area of the airport. But at the time of writing (1993) these are still proposals which will have to be the subject of Public Inquiries before they were implemented. Prospect Park on the other hand is already a practical proposition, permission for its development having been granted in 1992.

Part of the success in keeping the airport within its existing perimeter has been the policy of the local planning authority (first of Middlesex County Council and since 1965 of Hillingdon Council) of resisting planning applications connected with airport development. This was most recently (1991) reiterated in Hillingdon Council's draft Unitary Development Plan (26) which states " All activities directly connected with the airport will be expected to locate within its boundary..........Sites outside the airport will not therefore be regarded as available for the expansion of the airport or airport-related activities".

When, in 1990, British Airways first made a planning application to construct a Corporate Headquarters and Business Centre on land at Harmondsworth Moor the application was withdrawn in anticipation of a rejection. It would indeed have been surprising if it had been approved, not only because the proposal ran counter to the Hillingdon Council's stated policy on airport-related development but also because the site in question was in the Metropolitan Green Belt and formed part of the Colne Valley Regional Park.

Following withdrawal of the first application, British Airways entered into negotiations with Hillingdon Council to discuss modifications to its original proposals to improve the prospects of getting the development approved. As a result of these negotiations the company came up with a fresh set of proposals which went far beyond anything originally planned. These new proposals involved an undertaking on the part of British Airways to acquire an area of 109 hectares (270 acres) of land bounded on the south by the A4 (Colnbrook by-pass), on the west by the M25 motorway, on the north by the M4 motorway and skirting round Harmondsworth village on the east. In the south-east corner of this site the company proposed to develop 5.3 hectares (13 acres), more or less as originally, envisaged for its Corporate Headquarters and Business Centre. In return for being given permission to build their office block, British Airways undertook to purchase the remaining 104 hectares of land and to lay this out as public parkland to be known as "Prospect Park"

Although this proposal ran counter to Council policy as stated in its Unitary Development Plan, the revised scheme received favourable consideration from Hillingdon Council which, as it happened, owned about half of the total 270 acres of the land in question. Presumably the reason for the Council's attitude was that much of the land had been dug for gravel and, as a result of bad restoration, was lying derelict. This rather begged the question of why it had been allowed to become in this condition in the first place. As both landowner and local planning authority, Hillingdon Council and its predecessor authorities were uniquely placed to ensure, when granting permission for gravel extraction, that the land was restored to whatever condition that they liked to impose.

When the revised planning application by British Airways came before the Council for consideration the Council therefore expressed the view that "it was minded to approve it". It could not give outright approval but had to refer the matter to the Department of the Environment (DOE) because the development was a major departure from officially recognised policy on the Metropolitan Green

Belt. As a result of the referral, the DOE arranged for a Public Inquiry to be held which took place between 26 November and 11 December 1991. At the Inquiry British Airways application was vigorously supported by Hillingdon Council but opposed by neighbouring planning authorities and numerous local and environmental groups.

During the course of the Inquiry, Hillingdon Council announced that it had reached agreement to sell to British Airways the land in its ownership for the sum of £1.25 million. The Council also declared that, if approval for the development were to be given, it would use its compulsory purchase powers to obtain the areas of land, within the proposed park, not in its ownership and sell them on to British Airways.

In his report, which was published in October 1992, the Inspector (27) recommended that British Airways should be given permission to develop the site. He concluded that "There is no policy advice which would justify acceptance of BA's business case as so special as would justify development contrary to the Development Plan and there is no suggestion that BA's future would be put in jeopardy without a Corporate Business Centre at Prospect Park". But he then went on to say that "The most important consideration, in my opinion, is whether the environmental improvements leading to the establishment of a major informal recreation resource, open to the public, would justify the sacrifice of a part of the Green Belt". He concluded that the environmental benefits did outweigh the loss of Green Belt land for the office development and recommended that planning permission should be granted for the development.

The Inspector dismissed as conjectural the possibility that Prospect Park would be engulfed by a third runway but Figure 23 shows that it is a distinct possibility. Only the most gullible would believe that British Airways did not at least have this possibility in mind when it put the plan forward. The paranoic go further and allege that the acquisition is part of three-pronged attack by the aviation industry to extend the airport northwards up to the M4. The other two being the proposed fifth terminal and a possible third runway. This scenario is seen as having the following stages:

1) British Airways acquires permission to develop Prospect Park and goes ahead with the construction of its Corporate Business Centre.

2) BAA acquires permission to construct a fifth terminal on the Perry Oaks site.

3. BAA finds that the fifth terminal is under-used and to recover the costs of development claims that a third runway at Heathrow is essential.

4. A third runway is built that engulfs Prospect Park and consequently British Airways makes a huge windfall profit by selling Prospect Park to BAA. It acquired the land for less than £10000/acre; some idea of the possible profit it could make is provided by the fact that BAA will pay £500 million pounds to Thames Water to relocate the Perry Oaks sludge works which occupies a similar area to Prospect Park

5. The 50 percent increase in traffic generated by the runway is more than can be catered for by the fifth terminal so a sixth terminal is planned.

6. British Airways Corporate Headquarters becomes the sixth terminal.

A glance at Figure 23 shows how the various stages could so easily slot into place. Stage 1 has already occurred and Stage 2 is in the pipeline previous experience has shown that proposed developments at Heathrow are never what they seem to be.

What is not conjectural is the proposals, discussed later, to widen the M25 and the M4 motorways so even before any developments starts the edges of the "park" will have been shaved off.

Proposed Third Runway

As described on page 59, the first recent proposal for a third runway at Heathrow was made in 1987 by the Chairman of the Airport Transport User's Committee (ATUC). Although this is an official body the proposals were seen as merely the personal opinion of the Chairman and not one to be seriously considered. The proposal made by ATUC was for a relatively short runway close to the M4 motorway and running east-west between the M4 - Airport Spur Road and the M25. A map showing this location was printed as Figure 23 in the first print-run of this book but this has been replaced by a new Figure 23 which shows the latest proposals as described below.

In 1988 the Department of Transport asked the Civil Aviation Authority (CAA) for advice on the adequacy of UK airport capacity in the longer term, taking into account runway, terminal and airspace considerations. In July 1990, following consultations, the CAA reported that by 2005 another runway's capacity would be needed to serve the expected growth of air travel originating in the South East. It identified a number airports in and near the south east which had potential for further development but advised that, from the standpoint of the interests of users of air services, the preferred locations for new capacity were Gatwick, Heathrow and Stansted.

On publication of the CAA report the Department of Transport decided in November 1990 to set up a Working Group on Runway Capacity to Serve the South East (RUCATSE). This Group had responsibility to:

a) Evaluate the wider implications of developing additional runway capacity at the sites identified by the CAA.

b) Have regard to the considerations, including the environmental considerations, which led the Government in 1985 to the view that second runways should not be built at either Gatwick or Stansted; and to the relevance of those considerations at Heathrow and at other airports.

c) Test the CAA's conclusions on the contribution of regional airports and to gauge the extent to which these airports can play a part in meeting the overall demand into the next century.

In its initial deliberations RUCATSE assumed that a fifth terminal would be built at Heathrow even before BAA had made a formal application for its construction; confidently assuming the outcome of the Public Inquiry that will have to be held before T5 can be built. It drew up a short list of sites which it considered had the most potential for development. It dismissed the possibility that regional airports might play a significant role in alleviating the demand in the south east. In reaching this decision it ignored the fact that a person wishing to travel from say, Manchester to New Zealand, has first to travel to London and stay overnight in an airport hotel so that he can catch the flight from Heathrow. Because the traveller spent the night before the flight in the South East such a journey is regarded as having originated in the South East.

RUCATSE also initially refused to consider the possibility of constructing a completely new airport (to be called Marinair) in the Thames Estuary which has been proposed by a consortium of developers. Marinair would be built on sandbanks some seven miles off Sheerness. The advantages claimed are that it would be privately financed; it would be well positioned for Europe and the Channel Tunnel; it would eventually take more traffic than Heathrow does now; it would disturb no houses, no sleep and no people. These advantages led RUCATSE to concede that Marinair ought to be considered along with other proposals.

A RUCATSE sub-group which was set up to consider the environmental effects concluded, with only one dissension, that a third runway at Heathrow was unacceptable and proposed that Heathrow should be taken off the shortlist. However, the main RUCATSE committee, while acknowledging that a third runway at Heathrow would disturb 10 times as many people as any of the other options, did not accept this recommendation. It therefore decided to proceed with the further pursuit of Heathrow as a strong contender for the construction of an additional runway.

Figure 23 (which replaces the original Figure) shows the site proposed by RUCATSE for the possible construction of a third runway at Heathrow. This would take the airport boundary up to the M4 in the north, the M25 in the west and the River Crane in the east. It might also be added that these boundaries are remarkably like those in Figure 17 which were put forward in 1946 - the aviation Mafia is nothing if not persistent!

Figure 23 also shows that construction of a third runway would mean the total demolition of the four villages of Harlington, Sipson, Harmondsworth and Longford. The destruction of the villages would mean the demolition of 5500 houses and the eviction of some 10000 people from their homes. It would also mean that all the hotels and other commercial development along the Bath Road frontage and elsewhere in the affected area would be demolished. On architectural grounds the demolition of the hotels might be no bad thing but they would have to be replaced, no doubt by similar structures, on sites outside the expanded airport perimeter. There would also be many losses of buildings of architectural and historic importance. Longford and Harmondsworth are both designated Conservation Areas and the listed buildings destroyed would include the 12th Century Parish Churches of Harlington and Harmondsworth.

Apart from the extensive demolition involved the construction of a third runway would also mean a huge increase in the number of people affected by aircraft noise. Communities to the east and west at present hardly affected by noise would suddenly find themselves on a flight path.

The proposal, when taken into consideration with the consequent calamitous effects, is so preposterous that few people have taken it seriously. It has not therefore met with the resistance that might have been expected. Indeed the local MP for the affected area has categorically stated (28) that a third runway will never be built and has suggested that it is simply scaremongering on the part of his political opponents. This may be so but he cannot deny that RUCATSE exists and when, in a debate on the subject in the House of Commons, he asked for an assurance from the responsible Minister that a third runway would not be built at Heathrow, the Minister replied that he could not give an absolute assurance of the elimination of a third runway option (29).

In December 1992, in answer to a Parliamentary Question, the responsible Minister announced that RUCATSE would complete its work by mid-1993 In the form of a report which would set out the advantages and disadvantages of development of the sites on its short list. It is proposed to publish the report so that there could be full public consultation on RUCATSE's findings. The Minister added that it would ultimately be for the promoters rather than the Government to make specific proposals, which would in turn be subject to the normal planning processes.

The fifth terminal

In mid-1992 BAA put forward proposals for the construction of a fifth terminal at Heathrow. This would be built on the site of the Perry Oaks sludge works which would be re-located, at a total cost to BAA of £500 million, to an existing sewage works about one mile north-west of Perry Oaks. This sewage works is referred to by its owners, Thames Water, as Iver South although in reality it is south of the M4 motorway and much nearer to Colnbrook than it is to Iver.

The Iver South works, is very small compared with that at Perry Oaks. Before work could begin on the construction of a fifth terminal it would therefore have to be considerably extended in area and completely redeveloped. This cannot be done before planning approval has been given for the development, if this were not forthcoming the construction of the fifth terminal could not take place without another site being found for the sludge works.

Assuming that the sludge works were to be re-sited, BAA proposes that the fifth terminal would be built in stages. The first phase scheduled to open in 2002 would provide for 10 million passengers a year. The final phase, which would be completed by 2016, would bring the total capacity of the terminal to 30 million passengers a year.

When completed the fifth terminal would consist of a core building, three satellites, aircraft stands, aprons and taxiways, car parks, ancillary buildings and a hotel site. As discussed later, the complex would be linked to the M25 by a spur road. The time table for the complete programme is estimated to be:

1992 - Local consultations
1993 - Submission of planning application
1994 - Start of Public Inquiry
1995 - End of Public Inquiry
1997 - Government decision
Subject to planning permission being granted:
1997 - Start of construction
2001 - Completion of Phase 1 construction
2002 - Opening of Phase 1
2016 - Terminal reaches its maximum capacity

The BAA proposals have, of course, been challenged by the numerous pressure groups which are opposed to any further expansion of Heathrow. The reasons for the opposition are obvious, typical is the view expressed by Friends of the Earth - "Heathrow is the chosen airport to expand because it makes vast profits for BAA. Destroying the environment for their increased profits is not an option local people should have to accept". The environmental effects of airport expansion are discussed later in more detail.

Surface Access

Road.

The major motorway link for Heathrow is the M25 which was built to link together the other motorways around London. It was intended for longdistance traffic and was expected to carry 79000 vehicles/day by 2001. Some sections already take more than 200000, the majority of commuters travelling only for two or three junctions. In 1992 the Department of Transport published proposals to widen it to 14 lanes within 15 years by building parallel link roads alongside it. This would make it the widest motorway system in the world outside the USA. If a fifth terminal were to be built at Heathrow it would also be the busiest as BAA's intention is to construct a spur road to link the M25 directly to the terminal. In fact the Department of Transport has stated that, if approval to widen the M25 is not forthcoming, it would oppose the development of the terminal.

Rail.

The revised plans for a rail link from Paddington to Heathrow via a branch line from the airport to the Western Region main line at Hayes (see Figure 23 and page 61) gained Parliamentary approval in late 1991. The original timetable for its construction had been that Parliamentary approval would be given in mid 1990, work on the link would start in late 1990 and the new service would start in late 1993.

The hiatus in gaining Parliamentary approval, which could so easily have been avoided if the sponsors had listened to local objections, meant a delay of 18 months in the original timetable. This delay has been compounded by disagreements between the sponsors (BAA and British Rail) and work on the construction of the underground link between the BR mainline and the airport will not start until late 1993 at the earliest. It therefore seems unlikely that the link will be completed before 1997 - four years later than planned and nearly 50 years since proposals to provide a rapid rail link between the airport and central London were first made.

The rail link, when completed, will mean that it will be possible to travel from the airport to Paddington in about 16 minutes.

Environmental effects

Both BAA and British Airways constantly claim to be concerned about the effects that their activities have on the environment. BAA suffers from the delusion that it is environmentally responsible and a good neighbour of the local communities (30). Similarly British Airways has published an Environmental Review which states that its goal is "to be a good neighbour concerned for the community and the environment". Whether the neighbours would agree is, of course, a moot point and actions (quite literally in this case) speak louder than words.

It is, of course, fashionable for companies to express concern about the effects that their activities have on the environment. To be fair many companies do make genuine efforts to reduce the environmental impact of their operations.

Noise.

BAA claims that the huge increase in the proposed capacity of the airport (from 50 million to 80 million passengers/year) would not lead to a demand for a third runway or to a demand for an increase the number of night flights, or to an increase in noise levels. It gives as its reasons that the key to handling such a large increase in passengers, without a proportionate increase in flights, is the rising number of wide-bodied jets in modern airline fleets. It anticipates the introduction of even bigger jets, seating up to 800 people and claims that without Terminal 5 the airport would not be able to handle as many of these huge aircraft as the airlines might want to use.

The Government announced in February 1993 that it proposed to allow an increase in night flights from Heathrow to meet the existing demand. This was even before a formal planning application for the development of a fifth terminal was made. It therefore seems most unlikely that a fifth terminal would not increase pressures to allow night flying.

Air Pollution.

It is difficult to see how the huge predicted increases in road traffic and in air travel can be equated with the Government commitment to reduce the emission of carbon dioxide back to 1990 levels by the year 2000. Carbon dioxide is the major man-made contribution to the "green-house" effect which leads to global warming. When fossil fuels such as petrol and kerosene are burnt at maximum efficiency, water and carbon dioxide are the only combustion products and the only way of reducing emissions of carbon dioxide is to burn less fuel.

Improvements in engine design and efficiency will undoubtedly help to reduce emissions but are hardly likely to keep pace with the predicted increases in road and air traffic. In any case fuel costs are already a significant factor at the competitive margin for airlines so there is already a great emphasis on fuel efficiency. Furthermore, in practice, fuels are never burnt at 100 per cent efficiency so that, apart from carbon dioxide and water, other combustion products notably carbon monoxide, nitrogen oxides and volatile organic compounds (unburnt hydrocarbons) are also formed. In 1990 it was estimated that 90% of carbon monoxide, 51% of nitrogen oxides and 41% of volatile organic compounds emitted in Great Britain came from road traffic. Air transport has hitherto been considered to play only a minor role in air pollution but the pollutants are injected in the main at high altitudes where many of them have a more serious impact than lower in the atmosphere (31). A recent report 132) claims that air traffic over Europe is probably increasing the greenhouse effect as much as cars, power stations and shipping combined.

Carbon dioxide is part of the natural carbon cycle on which life on earth depends. Unless it is emitted in a confined space, carbon dioxide, arising from the combustion of fossil fuels, is not therefore in any way harmful to living organisms. For this reason it was not regarded as a pollutant until the recent concern about its contribution to the greenhouse effect. All the other combustion products have harmful effects on plants and animals and, in the form of acid rain, can damage buildings. Official surveys of nitrogen dioxide pollution and of ozone (formed by the interaction in bright sunlight of nitrogen oxides and unburnt hydrocarbons) show that on windless days in the summer months the maximum permitted levels are already frequently exceeded in London - the proposed expansion of the airport could only make matters worse.

Green Belt.

All the proposed developments to expand the airport would take place on land which forms part of the Metropolitan Green Belt. If they all came to fruition they would have the effect of removing the whole of the area south of the M4 and east of the M25 motorways from its present Green Belt designation. Most of this area is, of course, open land at present; it would not be in the Green Belt if it were not. This open land would be developed and all the buildings which lie within it would have to be demolished.

The demolitions would involve all the buildings in Harlington, Sipson, Harmondsworth and Longford including all the commercial development on the north side of the Bath Road. All the residential houses and most of the commercial property would have to be re-located nearby. The only possible location for these would be on Green Belt land outside the area taken up by the expanded airport. Apart from the demolition of existing buildings and their re-location elsewhere, the airport if expanded to the extent which is proposed would lead to extra demand for new development.

Even if no additional development took place, the overall effect would be equivalent to the construction of a New Town to accommodate at least 10000 people, 10 large hotels, several factories and warehouses of varying size and all the supporting infrastructure that these would require. There would therefore be an enormous loss, on an unprecedented scale, of Green Belt land which would mean that the built-up area of the western suburbs of London would extend, without a break, as far as Slough.

REFERENCES

(1) SHERWOOD P.T. and COX A.H. *Heathrow and District in Times Past.* Countryside Publications 1979.

(2) SHERWOOD P.T. and COX A.H. *More About Heathrow and District in Times Past.* Countryside Publications 1983.

(3) COBBETT William. *Rural Rides.* London 1853

(4) COTTON J., MILLS J. and CLEGG G. *Archaeology in West Middlesex.* Hillingdon Borough Libraries 1986.

(5) COTTON J. *Fern Hill: A Forgetten West Middlesex Earthwork.* Transactions of the London and Middlesex Archaeology Society 1990.

(6) ROY W. *Account of the measurement of a base on Hounslow Heath.* Royal Society Philosophical Transactions 1785 LXXV.

(7) MAXWELL G. *Highwayman's Heath.* Thomasons, Hounslow 1935.

(8) PUBLIC RECORD OFFICE (PRO). E178/1430/May 1587.

(9) SHERWOOD P.T. *Agriculture in Harmondsworth Parish. Its growth and decline 1800-1970.* West Drayton Local History Society 1973.

(10) WILLATTS E.C. *Middlesex and the London Region.* Report of the Land Utilisation Survey No.79.1937.

(11) ROWLANDS P. *The Duke of Northumberland's River.* The Honeslaw Chronicle Vol.10, No.2, Hounslow History Society 1987.

(12) ROYAL COMMISSION ON HISTORIC MONUMENTS. *An inventory of the Historic Monuments in Middlesex.* HMSO, London 1937.

(13) HAYTER George. *Heathrow - The story of the world's greatest international airport.* Pan Books, London 1989.

(14) PUBLIC RECORD OFFICE. Files listed principally under AVIA 2 and BT 217.

(15) BALFOUR H.H. *Wings over Westminster.* Hutchinson, London 1973.

(16) JAY D. *Change and Fortune : a political record.* Hutchinson, London 1980

(17) BUCHANAN C. *No way to the airport.* Longmans, London 1981.

(18) STAMP L. Dudley *Land Classification and Agriculture.* Greater London Development Plan 1944. HMSO London 1945.

(19) HUDSON K. and PETTIFER J. *Diamonds in the sky.* Bodley Head and BBC 1979.

(20) McKIE David *A sadly mismanaged affair.* Croom Helm, London 1973.

(21) MINISTRY OF HOUSING AND LOCAL GOVERNMENT. Post House Hotel appeal decision 28 March 1969. Reference APP/4418/A/31628.

(22) HALL Peter *Great Planning Disasters.* Weidenfeld and Nicholson, London 1983.

(23) GLIDEWELL I.D.L. *Report of the fourth terminal inquiry.* HMSO London 1979.

(24) EYRE Graham *The Airports Inquiries 1981-1983 (Expansion of Stansted: Fifth Terminal at Heathrow).* Report in nine volumes - no date or publisher given.

(25) COX J.E. Chairman's Introductory Speech. Air Transport Users' Committee Annual Press Conference 10 December 1987.

26. LONDON BOROUGH OF HILLINGDON. Draft Unitary Development Plan, April 1991

27. DEPARTMENT OF THE ENVIRONMENT. Prospect Park Appeal decision, 12 October 1992. Reference LRP219/R5510/02.

28. DICKS TERRY (Member of Parliament for Hayes and Harlington). Letter published in the "Hayes Gazette", March 11 1992.

29. House of Commons debate on Heathrow. Hansard, 23 June 1992, pp 235-242.

30. BAA, HEATHROW. Community Information Pack 1992.

31. BARRETT M. Aircraft Pollution - Environmental Impacts and Future Solutions. A World Wildlife Fund Research Paper 1991.

32. HAMER M. Polluting planes top the greenhouse league. New Scientist, 25 July 1992.

INDEX
Entries in bold type denote illustrations

Admiralty, The; 38
aerodromes;
    Great West **1**, **19**, 20, 22-23, 28, 35-39;
    Hawker's 19;
    Heston 18, 38, 41;
    White Waltham 38
agriculture; 18-20, 27, 30, 37, 40-41, 44, 61
aircraft; 16, 22, 34, 36, 40;
    Fairey Battle **1**;
    Lancastrian 47;
    military 38;
    model 22-23;
    noise 39-40
Aircraft Production, Ministry of; 38
Air Ministry; 22, 25-38, 41, **42-43**, 44-47, 58
    (see also Ministry of Civil Aviation)
Air Traffic; 55-56, 58
Air Transport User's Committee; 59
Albert Hall; 32
Anderson, Sir John; 36
Anglo Saxons; 13, 16
archaeology; 13-15
Ariel Hotel; 53, 55
Ash Cottage; **54**
Ashford County School; 28

BAA - see British Airports Authority
Baber Bridge; 28
Baillieu, Sir Clive; 38
Balfour, Harold; 35-36
Balfour, Lord of Inchrye - see Harold Balfour
Banks, Sir Joseph; 15
Banstead; 15
Baptist Church, Sipson; 26
barber; 27
baseline, (General Roy's); 15-**17**
Basham, Mr; 27
Bath Road; 9, 12-13, 18, 20, 24-25, 30-31, 37, 45-51, 53, 59, 61
Bathurst; 25
Battle of Britain; 28
Beaverbrook, Lord; 36
Bedfont; 27-28
Bedford Lodge; 53
Berkshire; 38
Best, Mr. & Mrs; 28
Biddescombe family; 25
Bing, George; 31

blacksmith; 33
Blagden, Charles; 15
BOAC - see British Overseas Airways Corporation
Bourne Avenue, Hayes; 61
Bragg's Way - see Tithe Barn Lane
brickearth; 12, 18, 40-41
British Airports Authority (BAA); 55,57-59,61
British Airways (BA); 38, 57
British Overseas Airways Corporation (BOAC); 46
British Rail; **60**-61
British South American Airways; 47
Broad Platt; 31
Brown, Charles; **1**
Brown Ernest; 36
Buchanan, Colin; 39
Bucks Advertiser; 31
Burton, Mr; 30

Caesar's Camp; **14**
Cain, Mr; 26
Cain's Farm House; 26
Cain's Lane; **1**, 20, 22, 24, 26-28
Cannon, King's Arbour 16, **17**, 25
Cars, parking; 53
Cedar of Lebanon; 25
Chessington; 16
Churchill, Winston; 41, 45-46
Coach and Horses Inn; 53, **55**
Cobbett, William; 12, 18
Colne River; 28, 31, 59
Common, The; 18, 26-27, 32
corn; 28
Covent Garden; 27
Crane River; 13, 28
Croft House; 26
Cryer, Mr; 26
Cublington; 50
Curtis, Mr; 27
Curtis, Harry; 28
cycle repairer; 27

daffodils; 27
Dance, George and Sons; 28
Dance, John; 27-28
Defence of the Realm Act; 37-39, 48
docks, London; 28;
Doghurst; 25
Doghurst Cottages; 25
Domesday Book; 16
Duke of Northumberland's River; 22-23, 28-**29**, 31

Dutch Barns; 25

earthwork; 13-15
Elizabeth I, Queen; 15
Enclosure - see Inclosure
Environment, Department of; 55
evangelism; 32
eviction (of inhabitants); 37, 41, 46, 48, 50
Eyre, Graham; 58

factories; 46
Faggs Road; 27
Fairey Aviation Company; 20-23, 28-29, 35-39;
    *airfield **19**;*
    Battle Bomber 1
Fairey, Sir (Charles) Richard; 23, 38-39
Fairview Farm; 31
Farms; 46;
    George Dance and Son's 28;
    Mr.Cain's 26;
    Fairview 31;
    Heathrow 28;
    *Heathrow Hall **25**;*
    John Heyward's 27;
    Patrick Howell's 25;
    Perry Oaks 20, **30**;
    Palmer's 26, 31;
    Perrott's 26-27;
    J.E.Philp and Son's 20;
    W. and S. Philp's 25-26;
    Mrs Sherwood's 27;
    Two Bridges 27-28;
    David and John Wild's 24, 32-33
Feltham; 20, 26-27
Fern Hill; 13
Field, Mr; 28
Flood, Mr; 25
flowers; 25-27, 32, 34
ford (across DNR River); 28
Forse, Mr; 25
Foulness; 55
    (see also Maplin Review Paper)
Fulham; 40

Gatwick Airport; 53, 55, 59-60
George III, King; 15-16
Gipsies; 31-33
Glover, Moses; 13
Goat House Tree Ford; 28
Goat House Tree Lane; 28

gravel; 11-12;
   digging 20, 31, 41;
   Taplow Terrace 12
Great South West Road; 44
Great West Aerodrome; **1**, **19**, 20, 22-23, 28, 35-39
Great West Staines Road; 35
Greater London Development Plan; 40
Green Belt; 53, 61

Hampton; 15
Hampton Court; 40
Hampton Poor House; 15
Harbour, Miss; 28
Harlington; 26, 44, 46, 48-50, 53, 61;
church 34, 48-49;
   Corner 47, 54;
   parish 13, 31
Harmondsworth; 15-16, 27, 44, 46, 49-50, 53, 59;
   aerodrome 20;
   church 26, 34, 50;
   forest 27;
   headmaster 25;
   Inclosure Award 15, 18, 26, 31;
   Inclosure Map 13;
   Manor of 18;
   Moor 59;
   parish 12 -13, 15-16, 18, 24, 27-28, 31-33;
   rate collector 25;
   Tithe barn 31
Hatton; 33
Hatton Cross; 27
Hatton Road; 33
Hayes; 22, 38, 61
Hayes Model Aeroplane Club; 23
Heathrow; **11-13**, 15-16, 18-20, 22-24, 26-28, 30-34;
   airport 13-14, 16, 18 20, 23-24, 35-46, **47-48**, 49, **50**, 51, 53-55, 57-59, 60, 61-62;
   Common 18, 26-27, 32;
   Common Barn 26-27;
    cottages **29**;
   Farm 28;
   Field 18;
   fifth terminal 38, 56-58, 61;
   fourth terminal 39, 55-56, 58;
   Hall 20, **25**-26, 31, 33;
   House 26;
   Master Development Plan 55;
   Mission Hall 26, 28;
   modern farmhouses **27**;
   ponds 31;
   Road 18, 20, 26, 31

Heston; 41;
    aerodrome 38
Heyward, John; 27
Hickmott, Miss; 28
High Tree Lane; 22, 28, 30
High Tree River; 28
    (see also Duke of Northumberland's River)
Hillingdon, London Borough of; 28, 55, 61
Home Counties; 36, 39
hops; 31
horses; 18
hotels;
    Ariel 53, 55;
    Ibis 54;
    Post House 53, 56;
    Skyways 53
Hounslow; 15, 26
Hounslow West; 60
Hounslow Heath; 12-14, 18, 26, 28, 30
houses, demolition of; 46, 48
House of Lords; 61
Howell, Patrick; 25
Hudson, Robert; 36

Ibis Hotel; **54**
Ice Ages; 11-12
Inclosure; 13, 15, 18, 26, 31
industries; agriculture 18-20, 27, 30, 37, 40-41, 44, 61;
    gravel digging 20, 31, 41;
    sludge disposal works 20, 37-38, 58
Ireland; 47
Iron Age 13
Isleworth; 13, 20, 28
Isleworth Mill; 28

Jackson, Joanna; 15
Jackson, Thomas; 15
Jay, Douglas; 36

Kew Gardens; 40
King family; 15
King's Arbour; 15-16;
    cannon 16, 25
Knapp, Mr.; 25

*Land Utilisation Survey; 18-***19**
Langley; 19
Lipscombe family; 28
London; 18, 24, 27, 31, 35-41, 46, 53, 55, 60;
    Diocese of 49

London Airport - see Heathrow Airport
Long Breakfast; 31
Longford; 16, 26, 28, 31, 33-34, 47
Longford River; 28
Loveridge; Betty; 32
Loveridge; Trainee; 32
Loveridge William; 32
Lysons, Rev. Daniel; 14

M4 motorway; 48, 53, 55-56, 59-61
M25 motorway; 57, 59-60
McKie, David; 53
Maidenhead; 40
Maplin Review Paper; 55-56
market gardening; 18, 25-28, 30, 36, 39-41
Maxwell, G.; 15, 24
Middlesex; 13, 27, 49
Middlesex Advertiser and Gazette; 44, 49-51
Middlesex Agricultural and Grower's Association; 20
Middlesex County Council; 20, 37-38
Ministry of Civil Aviation; 44-45, 47, 49-51
  (see also Air Ministry)
Mission Hall, Heathrow; 26, 28
Model Flying Clubs; 22
Mogden Sewage Works; 20, 58
mortuary; 25
Mudge, Captain; 16
Munich Crisis; 20, 26

Napoleon Bonaparte; 31
Newell Oliver; 33
noise (aircraft); 37, 39-40, 44-45, 53, 56, 59
North Hyde Road; 22
Northolt; 22
North West Essex and East Hertfordshire Preservation Association (NWEEHPA); 57-58

Old Oak Common; 28, 30
Old Magpies Inn; 25
orchards; 25-27, 30, 44
Ordnance Survey; 13, 16
Osterley Park; 40
Otercroft; 15
Paddington; 60-61
Paget family; 31
Paget, Thomas; 15
Palmer's Farm; 26,31
Parrott family; 26
Parrott, John; 26
Parrott, John Weekley; 26

Parrott, Martha; 26
Pease Path; 30-31
Perrott's Farm; 26-27
Perry Oaks; 18, 31, 47
*Perry Oaks Farm; 20, **30***
Perry Oaks Sludge Disposal Works; 20, 37-38, 45-46, 57-58
Philp, Fred; 31
Philp, J.E. and Son; 20
Philp, Josiah; 31
Philp, W.and S.; 25-26
Piccadilly Line; 60
pigs; 26-27, 30
Place, Mrs.; 26
Plough and Harrow Beer House; 27-28
*ploughing match; **19**-20*
police station, Harlington; 31
ponds; 25, 28, 31, 34
Poor House; 15
population (of Heathrow);
        eviction 37, 41, 46, 48, 50;
        re-housing 41, 44-45, 48, 50
*Post House Hotel; 53, **56***
Post Office; 26
Potter's Bar; 31
Public Record Office; 35
Pumpshire Gap; 30

railways;
        British Rail 60;
        Piccadilly Line 60
rate collection; 25
Rede, William; 15
rehousing of inhabitants; 41, 44-45, 48, 50
rhubarb; 25
Rising Sun Inn; 30
rivers; 11-13;
        Colne 28, 31, 59;
        Crane 28;
        *Duke of Northumberland's 22-23, 28, **29**;*
        High Tree 28,
        Longford 28
roads; 15, 28, 31, 48, 53, 55, 59-60
Rocque, John; 13
Roman Age; 14
Romanies - see Gipsies
Roskill Commission; 57
Ross, Reverend R.; 32
Roy, General William; 14-16;
        baseline 17
Roy Grove; 16

Royal Aeronautical Society; 21-22
Royal Air Force; 23, 35, 37, 47, 49
Royal Commission on Historic Monuments; 33, 49
runways; 14, 16, 22, 37, 39, 45-46, 55-56, 58-**60**

schools;
    Ashford County 28;
    Harmondsworth 25;
    Sipson 25
Schapsbury Hill; 13;
Shakesbury Hills; 13;
Shasbury Hill 13
Shepherd's Pool; 31
Sherwood, Mrs; 27
shops; 27-28
Sinclair, Sir Archibald; 45
Sipson; 16, 44, 46, 48-50, 59, 61;
    Baptist Church 26;
    Lane 61;
    school 25
Sipson House; 25
Skyways Hotel; 53
Smith, Bert; 32
Smith, Gipsy; 32
Smith, Lavinia; 32
Smith, Sarah; 32
Smith, Wisdom; 32
Southall; 61
Southall Gasometer; 28
South America; 47
Staines; 15
Staines Road; 15
Staines Rural District Council; 25
Stamp, L. Dudley; 40
Stansted; 36, 50, 56-59
Stanwell; 30, 34, 44
Strafford, Earl of; 31
Street, Arthur; 36
Stukeley, William; 14
Syon House; 28
Syon Park; 40

Technicolor factory; 30
Thames River; 11
Thames Valley; 11-12, 20
Thames Valley Market Gardening Plain; 18, 19, 20, 40
Thames Water Authority; 38, 58
Three Magpies Inn; 24-25
Tillier family; 26
Tithe Barn, Harmondsworth; 31

Tithe Barn Lane; 18, 19, 20, 31
tithes; 31
Transport, Department of; 58
triangulation; 16
Twickenham; 49
Two Bridges Farm; 27-28

Uttlesford District Council; 57
Uxbridge; 33

Vegetables; 26, 28, 30, 44

War Cabinet; 37, 46
Ward, Mr; 25
Waste Food Products Company; 27
Watkins and Simpson Seed Merchants; 27
Watkinson brothers; 26
Weekley, Henry; 30
Weekley, Rebecca; 26
Weekley Richard; 26, 30
West Bedfont; 27-28
West Drayton; 28, 44
Westland Helicopters; 38
    (see also Fairey Aviation Co.)
West London; 39
West Middlesex; 9, 13, 18, 20, 41
West Middlesex Main Drainage Scheme; 20
West Sussex County Council; 59
Wheatcut Corner; 26
White Waltham Airfield; 38
Whittington, Sidney; 30
Wild, David; 24,26, 33-34
Wild, John; 24,26, 32-33
Wild, William; 24
Wimpey, George Ltd; 47
Windsor; 39-40
Women's Land Army; 33
World War I; 33, 36
World War II; 20, 23, 26-27, 33, 35-39, 41, 45-46
Wrotham Park; 31